For my mother
wise, gentle, strong, tender, and loving

Future editions of this book will be a joint venture with you, the reader. If you have had an experience in an interview that hasn't been covered in these pages, or if you've had an experience that would serve as a good example for other interviewees, or if something bothers you that hasn't been covered here, write a letter about it to H. Anthony Medley, P.O. Box 9723, Marina del Rey, California, 90295. If your letter is quoted in the next edition of this book, you'll receive a free copy of that edition.

CONTENTS

It wasn't The Beatles' music that sold them to me; it was their charm.

George Martin, producer of
The Beatles' first record.

FOREWORD: 1992 UPDATE

When I first wrote *Sweaty Palms*, more than a decade ago, major East Coast publishing houses were skeptical. Typical was the reaction of Houghton-Mifflin who reviewed the manuscript and told me that their research department projected maximum sales of 2,000 copies.

But I wasn't some uninformed person hawking an idea about a book devoted entirely to the interview as a get-rich-quick scheme. I wrote the manuscript because I had founded a videotape interview service interviewing students at law schools for client law firms, and was conducting thousands of interviews. Interviewees would view me as someone who would not make a decision on them and, thus, after the taping sessions, would more often than not linger and question me about how they had done. Since I didn't have time to counsel them (and besides, this was not part of the service), I looked for a book to recommend. Although there were hundreds of books on the interview written for the *interviewer*, there was nothing written for the *interviewee*. So, Houghton-Mifflin and the other East Coast behemoths to the contrary notwithstanding, I knew the marketplace and what was needed. And *Sweaty Palms* was it—a book devoted entirely to interviews and written from the interviewee's point of view.

Now, with more than 300,000 copies sold, and sales increasing every year, *Sweaty Palms* has not only proven itself in the marketplace, it has received the sincerest form of flattery, imitations galore, which appear and disappear with regularity. Some, however, deserve comment because of the harm they do by giving the reader specific answers to specific questions to use in interviews.

I can't believe that anyone who has actually conducted a selection interview could conceive in his wildest imagination of worse advice for an interviewee than to memorize specific answers to give to questions that an interviewer might ask. There are several reasons for this:

1. There's nothing that will turn an interviewer off faster than hearing a memorized answer recited by rote.

2. How many times must an interviewer hear the same answer before getting suspicious that the interviewee is not answering the questions, but parroting words that some consultant drafted? More than twice?

3. One of the prime purposes of an interview is to get an honest exchange. The interviewee must come across as honest or failure is certain. Yet what could be more dishonest than answering an interviewer's question with *someone else's answer?* Once the interviewer determines that that is happening, your chance of getting an offer will be reduced to virtually zero.

You don't need to just take my word for this. Joseph Alibrandi, president and chairman of the board of Whittaker Corporation, and winner of the UCLA School of Management's Man of the Year award, told me, "If there's one thing in an interview that's important to me, it's that I see the real person, not some guy who's playing a role that some search consultant has advised him on—how to sit and how to talk and all that—because I see through that in five minutes and it's pathetic."

So one thing you *will not* get in *Sweaty Palms* is canned answers to commonly asked questions. If that's what you want, don't buy Sweaty Palms.

What you *will get* is specific and detailed information about the interview itself, what to expect, how to prepare, and how to provide yourself with the confidence and knowledge to answer *any* question the interviewer asks from your own experience and in your own words.

If that's what you want, read on.

THE INTERVIEW

A candidate I once interviewed for a secretarial position could type 90 words per minute and take shorthand at 120 words per minute. She was presentable and had good references. But in addition to showing up ten minutes late, she called me " Mr. Melody" throughout the interview. The two main things I remembered about her were that she had kept me waiting and that she had constantly mispronounced my name. I finally offered the position to someone whose typing and shorthand skills were not nearly as good.

More often than not, it is the small things that occur in an interview that spell the difference between getting an offer and being rejected. As you will learn as you read on, the basic objective of a candidate in an interview is to spark a positive felling in the interviewer. It's a purely subjective feeling, so your close attention to little things is essential.

The basics

Be certain of the time and place of the interview and the name of the interviewer. Sometimes candidates are so excited to get an interview that they neglect to ask for this essential information. Write it down and keep it with you until after the interview. If no one tells you your interviewer's name, ask. Sometimes the situation precludes finding out, but you're ahead of the game if you know it going in.

Arrive early for the interview. If you plan on arriving at least fifteen minutes before the appointed time, you will have a cushion against unforeseen delays, such as a traffic tie-up or an elevator breakdown or an inability to find the right building or office, any of which could cause you to be late if you depended on split-second timing. Being early can also give the interviewer a good initial impression of your reliability and interest.

Bring a pen and notebook with you. The notebook should fit in a pocket or purse so that you don't walk into the interview room with it in hand. Its purpose is twofold. First, the interviewer may give you some information to write down. If you're prepared with your own writing material you won't have to interrupt the interview to hunt down paper and pen.

Second, immediately after the interview you should make notes on what occurred during the interview and what your reactions were to the interviewer. This information can be very important in future interviews so that your replies remain consistent. Further, if you have many different interviews, your notes will help your recall of each and aid in making a choice in jobs, should that become necessary. Don't, however, make notes during the interview unless the interviewer asks you to write something down.

Remember the interviewer's name. There is possibly no sweeter sound to the human ear than the sound of one's own name. If you don't learn the interviewer's name prior to the interview concentrate on it when introduced and remember it. For some people this is very difficult. They are concentrating on themselves so much and thinking about how nervous they are that they completely forget the name or don't pay close attention when they hear it for the first time.

The best thing to do is to repeat the name immediately after the introduction by saying something on the order of "How do you do, Mr. (or Ms.) Smith." Then repeat the name a couple of times during the first part of the interview. This repetition will help you remember the name. It will also have a pleasing effect on the interviewer.

Reader Joseph D. Lee of El Cerrito, California, writes about the importance of properly pronouncing an interviewer's name:

I recently had an interview for admission to a particular academic program; roughly one in three applicants met, as did I, with success. My interviewer had a Spanish surname, and I have the good fortune to have learned to speak Spanish well. I also had the good fortune to have heard the interviewer speak previously, so that I was certain that he was bilingual.

When I introduced myself to him, I pronounced his name as it would be pronounced in Spanish, rather than English (there is quite a difference!). The interviewer's response was notably positive. "You pronounce my name like you speak Spanish," he said, and immediately we were off to a friendly discussion of how I learned Spanish, how I hoped to be able to use it in the program, and the like. My pronunciation of his name not only opened the conversation on a positive note, it conveyed a sense of respect for another's language and culture. Thus I believe that this beginning was central to the success of my interview.

A similar point should be made about difficult names: those who possess them are frequently either proud of them or mortified by them. In either case, pronouncing them correctly can only be a plus. And of course there are many ways to ascertain the correct pronunciation of an interviewer's name: call his receptionist or secretary anonymously; check with the job placement director, if the interview has been arranged by another; or ask someone who speaks Greek, Spanish, or whatever.

3

One caveat: Do not call the interviewer by his or her first name unless invited to do so (which is unlikely). Calling people by their first names without being asked is a familiarity that offends a great many.

Remember Christ's parable comparing the guest at a wedding feast who took a seat near the head of the table and was embarrassed by being asked to move farther down while the guest who sat at the lowest place was honored by being asked to move up. You have nothing to lose by addressing your interviewer formally as "Mr." (or Ms., Miss, or Mrs.), and nothing to gain by calling your interviewer "Charlie" or "Shirley." If your interviewer is a woman, notice whether she's wearing a wedding ring. If not, I recommend calling her "Ms." If she's sympathetic to the feminist ideology, it could be a plus for you, whereas calling her "Miss" may offend her. On the other hand, if she is not supportive of feminist beliefs, calling her "Ms." should not offend her as much as calling her "Miss" could offend someone who is sympathetic.

Don't offer to shake hands unless the interviewer offers a hand first. I was raised by my mother to obey the old rule of polite society that a gentleman does not offer his hand to a lady unless she offers her hand first. But as an interviewer, I always offer to shake hands, whether the interviewee is male or female. I am initially trying to put the interviewee at ease, and a handshake is a good way to break down some barriers.

But interviewers are different. Some will not offer to shake hands. A male interviewee should not offer to shake hands if his interviewer does not first offer. For a woman, this is not so crucial. You may find a chivalrous interviewer who believes it is offensive for a man to offer his hand to a woman but would not be offended for a female interviewee to initiate the handshake. The safe rule, in any event, is not to offer your hand unless the interviewer makes the first move.

If you do shake hands, make it a firm grip. A weak handshake can be a real turnoff. But don't go overboard and give your Superman grip. If you take the interviewer to the floor with your hearty handshake, you won't be remembered with good feelings.

Don't smoke unless invited. Many people are allergic to cigarette smoke. Further, the interviewer may have to occupy the room for the entire day, and doesn't want it filled up with smoke. Smoking has generally become so controversial that you shouldn't take the chance of offending by lighting up without being invited. No matter how addicted you are to tobacco, you should be able to survive a few minutes without your dose. Many nonsmokers have an almost religious antagonism to smoking. Why risk offending?

Don't chew gum. Gum chewing can communicate a distinctly negative impression. It may not offend some interviewers, but it is still better not to take the risk.

Wait for your interviewer to sit down or invite you to sit down before seating yourself.

Most of these suggestions are items of common courtesy, but they are often overlooked, particularly in the context of the interview when you are nervous and thinking about yourself.

It is a keystone of any effective interview for you to come across as an honest person. "Here I am with all my warts" is the impression that is best to leave. You don't want to expound on your warts, but you want to leave the impression that you accept yourself for what you are and that you want the interviewer to know you as the person you are.

But that's just the *impression* you want to leave. You must attune yourself to the interviewer early, and this requires strict attention to him and his reaction to you. (Let's assume, for the balance of this chapter, that the interviewer is male.) You will have to make some very astute judgments in the early moments of the interview, so you must concern yourself with the interviewer's problems, prejudices, desires, and feelings. If the interviewer is a dynamic, take-charge sort who wants to regale you with stories, go along with it. If the interviewer is somewhat shy and insecure, help him out. If the interviewer exhibits any prejudices that you are able to perceive, don't run afoul of them. You must exercise the perception to categorize the interviewer early and then the discretion to guide the interview along the lines that help him arrive at the conclusion you wish.

Being interviewed and being interviewed well are two entirely different matters.

You must sell yourself

As an interviewee you are primarily a seller. The product you are selling is yourself, and the assets of the product consist of your experience, skills, and personality. You communicate your experience and skills in your résumé, but your personality comes across in the interview.

You must recognize that you are in a selling situation and that it is your goal to arouse the interest of the interviewer in you. If you wait expectantly for questions and dutifully answer them, you have done nothing to distinguish yourself from the hundreds of other interviewees who will be encountered.

Paul Ivey, in his classic *Successful Salesmanship*, states, "There is one sure-fire way of arousing their interest . . . : find out what they are already interested in and then talk about it. If you talk about what they are interested in, they will later on be willing to consider what you are interested in."

Techniques for selling yourself

A large part of an interview is you as the interviewee selling yourself to the interviewer. Therefore it's well to know the techniques of selling.

The basic goal of an interview for selection is to determine personality traits. In *Successful Salesmanship*, Paul Ivey breaks the personality of a good salesman into four categories. The first is **enthusiasm**, which is so important that all of Chapter 4 is devoted to this single aspect. The other three are sincerity, tact, and courtesy.

Sincerity

Sincerity goes hand in hand with enthusiasm. If you generate a phony enthusiasm for something, such as a job about which you know nothing, two judgments may be made, both negative. First, the interviewer may conclude that you're so hard up for a job that you'll take anything and he may reject you on that basis. Or he may conclude that your enthusiasm is insincere, which indicates a trait of dishonesty. Dishonesty, whether it is gleaned through lying or insincerity, can be grounds for immediate termination of consideration. For this reason you should reserve your enthusiasm for something in which you are genuinely interested.

Tact

Ivey's third facet of personality is **tact**. Most good interviewers will bring up a controversial subject or interject stress into an interview by saying something with which he knows you'll disagree. How you handle this situation is a main test of the interview.

To disagree with tact, your response must first agree, then disagree. For example, you may say, "Yes, I see what you mean, but . . . " or, "That's a good point. On the other hand . . . " If the agreement does not precede the disagreement, your answer will not have been tactful.

Courtesy

The fourth aspect in Ivey's analysis of the personality traits required of a good seller is **courtesy**. A lack of courtesy will probably be disastrous to the interview. You can be discourteous to the interviewer in many ways: in the way you dress, in the way you speak, in the way you ask questions, in the way you stand and sit, in the way you shake hands. If you arrive late for an interview dressed in a slovenly or unkempt manner, you are showing a lack of courtesy. If you slouch or are inattentive, your lack of courtesy will be noted. The use of profanity or telling of obscene jokes may be received as a lack of courtesy.

Courtesy is consideration of the feelings of others. Unfortunately society today seems to be moving in the direction where a lack of courtesy is the norm. "Doing your own thing" implies a disregard of one's obligation to others. If you are a truly courteous person, you will think of how your actions will affect others before you act. Displaying a lack of this consideration will not result in "admiration" for your "independence." Rather, it may result in your leaving the impression of being a boor and could terminate any chance you might have had for further consideration.

In addition to Ivy's four points, I would add a few tips of my own, all of which come under the general heading of . . .

Keeping the interviewer's attention

Boredom is invariably an element of interviewing. If you add to the boredom, you're putting nails in your coffin. Shortly after John F. Kennedy was elected president, he had decided upon a farm leader to be his secretary of agriculture and invited the candidate to his Georgetown apartment for an initial interview. "It was so boring," he said later, "and the living room was so warm, that I actually fell asleep." The candidate was quickly rejected.

An interviewer will ask the same questions of people with similar interests and backgrounds and receive the same answers. One of the better techniques of good interviewing is to break that boredom and routine by getting interviewers to talk about something that interests them.

If you talk intelligently about something in which the interviewer is concerned, he will be more interested in you. Interviewers are like everyone else: they are selfish, and their own concerns are paramount in their minds. If you show a genuine interest in these concerns and can discuss them intelligently, the interest in you will be sparked. You need to be careful, though. If you are unable to communicate your interest with sincerity, the likely consequence will be a loss of confidence in you, and you'll be worse off than when you started.

Pay strict attention to how you are being received by the interviewer. If you determine that interest is lagging, there are a few tricks you can use to bring it back around.

You can vary the tone of your voice (for example, by lowering it or making it louder). Television advertisers often do this by making commercials louder than the show they sponsor. Theoretically this change in tone beckons and makes viewers more attentive to something they may have little desire to hear.

You can vary the tempo at which you speak (by speeding it up or slowing it down). Essentially any change that you make from the manner in which you had been behaving will act as a lure to bring the interviewer's attention back from its wandering. You must capture and retain the interviewer's interest, or the remainder of the interview will be a mere formality and probably result in rejection.

What you do with that attention once you capture it will determine whether your interview is going to be successful. If, for example, you convince the interviewer that you don't have the experience for the job or the skills required or that your personality is abrasive or bland, you're no better off then you were before you walked in the door.

Once you have captured his attention, you must continue selling yourself and create the desire in the interviewer to have you as an employee.

Paul Ivey says that "desire . . . rests on conviction; and the former cannot be created without the latter. . . . The intelligent salesman adjusts his sales talk to the customer's system of beliefs; his ideas enter the customer's mind unpercepted because they are so similar to the customer's own ideas. There is no customer-resistance, but rather customer-assistance. There is agreement instead of disagreement." Your preparation and perception thus become important bases. If you have researched the interviewer (in ways discussed in the next chapter), you know enough to make some initial judgments as to what kind of person you will be encountering. If you know his background you may be able to make some intelligent guesses as to his interests and beliefs. But before you act on these assumptions, you must make some evaluations during the initial part of the interview. And if you're coming into the interview with no advance preparation, these early evaluations will be all that you have to go on.

If you can get the interviewer to reveal something personal in an early part of the interview, you can reinforce or verify some of your assumptions before you act on them. The first part of the interview is often a jousting period in which you feel each other out. What you must realize is that the interviewer probably assumes that you are the typical interviewee who will meekly sit and wait for him to conduct the interview. Therefore, he will not be prepared for subtle probes.

You must take your key from the interviewer. If he starts boldly by asking questions and gives you no signal that personal queries will be entertained, you have to wait until the time is propitious. On the other hand, if he is relaxed, self-confident, and interested, you don't have to worry too much. And if you can get him to talk about himself with interest, you will have several advantages. First, this will give you information you can use as the interview progresses. Second, everyone likes to talk about themselves and if you're interested and communicate that interest, the positive feelings you're trying to create will be enhanced. Third, you'll have a better chance to find areas of common interest and areas of possible conflict to avoid.

If you get the chance, and if he seems to invite it, ask a few personal questions. Is he married? Does he have any children? Play tennis or golf? Listen to Bach, Neil Diamond, or Madonna? Ever been to Katmandu? If you can discover something in common, you will be way ahead of the game.

Some interviewers can react negatively to such probing, so you have to do it in a natural, conversational way. But just think. How would you feel if the highlight of your life was when you ice-skated on the Bering Straits and suddenly you're interviewing someone who did the same thing. Would you be inclined to offer her a job? Is grass green?

If you are unable to penetrate the shield, you can still make some educated guesses about the interviewer's orientation and proceed on that basis. For example, if you have submitted your résumé in advance and then been called in for an interview, you may safely assume that the interviewer has already determined that you are qualified for the position, based upon the data you provided. You may then proceed to work upon this belief by verifying and amplifying the facts on your résumé and by detailing specific experience and skills.

You can also assume that the interviewer knows what he wants out of the position, and you may ask how he views the position and what tasks it entails. After discussing this, you can describe your experience and skills to exact specifications.

It's important that you get some kind of a job specification from the interviewer early in the interview so that you can key what you can accomplish to what he wants accomplished. If you get into a detailed discussion of your skills and experience before you've had a chance to probe what he's looking for, you're adrift in a world of unknowns.

Some interviewers will tell you something about the job before they start questioning you, but most won't. Most interviewers are inwardly oriented, just as are most interviewees, and they may not really focus on the interviewee. They may be thinking instead about asking the right questions in the interview. Therefore, if you can easily segue into questioning him about the position early on, you may discover some valuable keys that you can use to guide the rest of the interview and create the realization that you are the right person to fill the position.

When the interviewer identifies with you

If you can strike a responsive chord in the interviewer by having him conclude that the two of you think alike, you will have gone a long way toward creating the feeling in him that can result in an offer, as the following incident illustrates.

Robert A. Lovett was described by David Halberstam in *The Best and the Brightest* as "the symbolic expert, representative of the best of the breed ... a man of impeccable credentials, indeed he passed on other people's credentials, deciding who was safe and sound, who was ready for advancement and who was not." Charles B. (Tex) Thornton was the founder, chairman of the board, and chief executive officer of Litton Industries, the pioneer conglomerate, a man of immense wealth and power, and at one time the nominal chief of staff of the captains of industry in the United States.

One day in 1941, these titans met for the first time. Lovett was then assistant secretary of war and Thornton was a twenty-seven year old, $4,600-a-year statistician for the U.S. Housing Authority in Washington. Young Thornton had written a report that had interested Lovett, and Lovett wanted to meet him. Thornton telephoned for an appointment and found himself still waiting in Lovett's outer office long after the appointed time. Having run out of time, he rose to leave, when Lovett's secretary persuaded him to wait a few minutes longer, an act that Thornton has said changed the whole course of his life.

After Lovett arrived, he and Thornton talked. The more the youthful Thornton spoke, the more Lovett liked him. Lovett was a banker who had a love affair with figures and Thornton talked of numbers as if they were a language of their own. This impressed Lovett immensely. Here was a man in his own mold! Not only that, but Thornton was not intimidated by Lovett's authority. Lovett was looking for just such a person.

Thornton was prepared. He spoke the technical language, and he revealed that he knew what he was talking about. He was respectful of the man and the office of Lovett but communicated his respect in himself so that he was not obeisant. He was not intimidated by Lovett or his office. He met Lovett as an intellectual equal, while deferring to the office and experience of the older man. Thornton ignited a feeling in Lovett and Lovett hired him. From that point, Thornton was associating with the powers that ran the World War II logistical effort. He built a reputation that enabled him to negotiate a lucrative contract for himself and several colleagues with Hughes Aircraft after the war and finally left Hughes to found Litton and his own fortune. He traces his success to this interview with Lovett. Had he not impressed Lovett sufficiently the world may never have heard of Tex Thornton.

Lovett later said that Thornton reminded him of himself in the way he spoke about figures. Thornton came across in the interview as a man of unusual intellectual capability, but having Lovett identify so personally with Thornton was the essential element in the entire interview.

If you can make an interviewer see another him in you, you will have won him over.

Lovett saw that Thornton thought as he did and identified with him. Without question, Lovett made a conclusion based upon the "halo" effect of this feeling. (The halo effect is discussed in Chapter 14.) Thornton continued to perform, but this one impression that he created during the interview got him his chance.

Think about the interviewer

Don't think about yourself so much. Most interviewers think about themselves to the exclusion of everyone else. When you walk into a room, you may be worrying about how you look, whether your palms are sweaty, whether your voice will crack.

But we all think about ourselves, and the interviewer is no exception. Maybe he doesn't have the same insecurities, but he's thinking about himself all the same. He might be worried about his job or making the plane that night. Or the problem could be an ill child, an unfaithful spouse, or an argument with the boss. There may be a million things on the interviewer's mind other than you.

So there you are worrying about yourself and your sweaty palms and there he is thinking about something else. In fact, the interviewer may have the same insecurities. He may not have conducted many interviews and be worried that he's going to make a fool of himself. He may even be worried that his palms are sweaty. Or, worse, if he is really inexperienced, he may feel that he won't be able to think of anything to say and there will be gaps of silence.

Whatever his thoughts, there's a good possibility that he's not thinking what you think he's thinking. He's not taking you apart piece by piece in his mind, cooly evaluating your every movement.

Who controls the interview?

An interviewer can be expected to control the **flow** of the interview. Some may begin by asking general questions to ease your nervousness and will then move on to more specific questions about areas in which they are interested that are not covered on your résumé. But, although the interviewer controls the flow of the interview, the interviewee controls the **content**. After all, an interview generally consists of an interviewer's asking questions and you answering them. What you do with the questions is up to you. Thus you should go into the interview knowing the points you want to cover—for example, your achievements.

If you run into such a situation where he is insecure and unsure of himself try to make the interview go as smoothly as possible for him. If you do and you control the interview to the extent that there are no gaps and you say what you want to say, you will have probably conducted a very good interview.

If you go into the interview thinking about the interviewer, you will relieve yourself of the tremendous tension that most interviewees feel about an interview. You will feel that you have some control of the situation and a plan of attack.

As a student I once entered an interview room at the end of a warm spring day, and the interviewer was standing with his back to me staring out the window. It was obvious that he was bored to tears. He had had twenty-five interviews with students who were carbon copies of one another, and he had a few more to go with the same monotonous questions and answers.

I had just heard some news on the radio, so before he could start his routine of questions, I asked, "Did you hear that Khrushchev was overthrown?"

His eyes lit up, and we spent several minutes talking of Russia, which we had both visited. Suddenly his routine was broken, and right off the bat we had something in common. I was invited to see his firm and, although I didn't take a job with them, the interview was a success because I thought about breaking his boredom rather than worrying about whether my pants were pressed.

CHECKLIST

★ Write down the time and place of the interview and the name of the interviewer.

★ Arrive early for the interview.

★ Bring a pen and notebook with you.

★ Write a synopsis of the interview immediately afterward.

★ Remember the interviewer's name.

★ Don't offer to shake hands unless the interviewer offers a hand first.

★ Don't smoke unless invited.

★ Don't chew gum.

★ Wait for the interviewer to sit down or invite you to seat yourself before you sit down.

★ Present yourself as an honest person; do not try to hide anything.

★ Remember you're selling yourself.

★ Remember to combat the interviewer's boredom.

★ Be outwardly oriented.

★ Retain the interviewer's attention by varying the tempo of your speech and the tone of your voice.

★ Get the interviewer to talk about himself early.

★ Get him to give you a job specification early in the interview.

★ Remember your goal is to strike a good feeling in him about you.

★ The interviewer will control the **flow** of the interview.

★ You must control the **content** of the interview.
★ Don't think about yourself so much.
★ Recognize the insecurities of the interviewer.

PREPARATION

       A hit Broadway show consists of two and a half hours of entertainment, but it is the culmination of endless weeks of rehearsal and hard work to prepare the finished performance. A ballerina started taking lessons at the age of six to accomplish that pirouette that seems so effortless when she's twenty-one. The basketball player started shooting baskets when he was nine to perfect that jump shot he nets with seeming ease when he's twenty-five.

    If we want to do something well, we spend a disproportionate amount of time preparing for it compared with the time it takes to perform the actual deed. Being interviewed should be no different. But the typical interviewee will spend hours and hours to get an interview, then figure that the interview will take care of itself. Beyond dressing a little more carefully than usual, the interviewee won't spend any further time or effort preparing for it.

The reason interviewees act this way is based upon the misperception that the interviewer will know exactly what she wants to get out of that interview (for this chapter, let's assume the interviewer is a woman) and will ask the questions she needs in order to arrive at the answers she seeks. Thus, the interviewee thinks, what can I do to prepare? I don't know what she is looking for. I'll just go to the interview and answer her questions.

Unfortunately the vast majority of interviewees don't realize that it is up to them to control the content of the interview. Remember that you are the seller and the product you are selling is yourself. You should not leave it up to the interviewer to probe wildly for areas of concern. If you are savvy, you'll gently lead the interviewer to your strengths. The primary element in controlling the interview is to be prepared; and the most important part of preparing is getting to know yourself.

Your past is prologue

One thing to realize is that the older you are and the more you've been around, the more you are inescapably wedded to your past. "What's past is prologue" is a rule that most selection interviewers follow. If you have a history of personality conflicts with supervisors, the conclusion will be that this problem will not change. If you have a history of missing a lot of work for sickness, this will be considered in evaluating your future performance. If you are late often, this will be considered. You should be aware of any of these traits you possess. One of your objectives will be to establish a rapport with the interviewer so that she can accept these defects, either with a plausible explanation as to why they are not your norm or by convincing her that your assets—be they motivation, ambition, intelligence, personality, or leadership—far outweigh your track record of defects.

This is where your preparation will be most important. If you know yourself and you know that your defects will be revealed, you must prepare the interview so that you know how to downplay your defects and sell your assets. The more defects that you have that are revealed on your record, the more important it is that you control the interview so that the discussion is geared toward your strengths and away from your weaknesses.

How well do you know yourself? Do you remember what you've done in the past? That sounds pretty easy doesn't it? Of course you remember what you've done. Think so? How many times have you seen a long-lost friend and been reminded of an episode in your past which you hadn't thought about in years? Do you think you would have thought of that episode had your friend not jarred your memory?

Being interviewed consists in part of being deft in the conservational art. You are what you have done. In order to realize what you are, you must remember what you have done and be able to relate it. If you don't remember it, you won't be able to relate it. Further, you may misconstrue what you are.

Write a diary

The best way to begin to get to know yourself is to write the story of your life, your autobiography. It requires dedication and a great deal of time, but it can help you gain insights into yourself.

To do it properly, it should be written chronologically. Start at the beginning and go through each year, setting down incidents as they occurred. Don't be afraid to get help. If you remember someone from your past who participated in something with you but your memory is a little fuzzy, contact them for their recollections. This will not only help you in remembering what happened, it may trigger other memories.

This can run into hundreds of pages and tens of thousands of words, but when you're done, you'll have a compendium of your experiences. You can use it to make a good assessment of who you are and what you have to offer, and it will be a ready reference of things about which you may wish to speak to an interviewer. Additionally, and maybe even more importantly, it may trigger clues about things you wish to avoid discussing with an interviewer.

Once you have your story down on paper, you have to come to grips with two things: what you want and what you have to offer. What you want can be subdivided into how much money you want and what kind of work you want.

What will make you happy

The second element you must analyze is what you want to do. What kind of job will make you happy? Only you can answer this. Some people are happy if they spend the entire day typing. That would drive others up the wall. Some are happy selling brushes door to door. Others would sink to the depths of depression if they had to do that. Some are happy if they have a lot of responsibility. Others want to avoid responsibility.

One of the best ways to determine the elements of a job you want is to write two lists, one consisting of the things you enjoy in a job and the other consisting of the things you don't enjoy. Make these lists as complete as possible. You won't be able to do this in one sitting. You may remember something while you're doing your marketing or are watching a baseball game. Whenever you think of a new element for one of the lists, write it down immediately; otherwise you may forget it. Then it'll not only be gone, but it can drive you crazy trying to remember it.

Once you have this list fairly complete, you should have a good job specification in terms of salary and function. It will give you a list of questions you know you will want to ask your interviewer. It will also give you the confidence that the interview is a two-way street; both you and the interviewer are interviewing each other.

Desires versus requirements

Finally, divide the list containing the elements you enjoy in a job into two categories, one containing the items you must have and the other containing the items you like but don't need. This is essential because the odds are that you're not going to find a job that contains everything you want.

You may find a good position but it's on the fortieth floor and you hate elevators, or it's next to a chain-smoker and you're allergic to cigarette smoke, or it's located in Kansas and you love the ocean. Before you go into your interview, know the things that you must have and those that you can do without in a pinch. Maybe you can forgo seeing the ocean or can overcome your fear of elevators. Maybe you can't. If you can't, know it going in. But don't get yourself in a position of turning down the job in Kansas and later regretting it, realizing that the job was more important to you than the ocean.

Your list of requirements should be short. If it's not, you are going to find yourself in the job market for a long, long time because most jobs fall short of being ideal.

Research the company

Learn as much as you can about the company you will be interviewing. If you were in sales, you wouldn't dream of going into a presentation without knowing something about the business of the potential customer. You would tailor your sales pitch to the needs of that business. If you were going to make a speech, you would want to know as much about the audience as you could so that you could direct your speech to the areas of the audience's interests. Similarly, when you go into an interview, you should know as much about the company as possible so that you can train your approach toward making the interviewer feel that you fit the requirements of the job.

The impression left by your preparation is sometimes subtle, but it is invariably positive. If, for example, you are interviewing a bank and have a working knowledge of what the bank does, this knowledge will come across to the interviewer. Conversely, if you are ignorant of the bank's business, it will register as a definite negative.

Interviewers are looking to determine not only your interest in obtaining a job but in working for their company, rather than some other one. If you've taken the initiative to find out what the company does, it indicates that you have done some homework. If you don't have the interest to find out what kind of work the company does prior to the interview, that lack of interest may be quickly discovered by the interviewer. Not only can you expect to be thrown for a loss by some questions asked by the interviewer, but she may draw a distinctly negative impression from your apparent lack of interest.

Interviewers will invariably ask you what you think you can add to the company as an employee. How can you answer if you don't even know what the company does? Whether you have done this basic amount of research will come out in other ways. For example, most interviewers will reach a point where they ask you if you have any questions about the company or its operations. This may seem to be a maneuver to turn the interview over to you, but in fact it's a very potent question. From the questions you ask, the interviewer can determine how much you know of the company and for what reasons, if any, you would like to work for it.

How to research the company

How do you research the company? College placement offices are excellent sources of information. They are generally responsive to requests for information, whether or not you're a student or alumnus, although their policies differ in accordance with the personality of the person running the office. They are good places to start, and if the inquiry does result in rejection, you haven't lost anything.

There is a myriad of publications to which you may refer. Some of these include:

Better Business Bureau reports
Chamber of Commerce publications
College Placement Directory (Zimmerman & Lavine)
College Placement Annual (College Placement Council)
Dun & Bradstreet Reference Book
Fitch Corporations Manuals
Moody's Manuals
MacRae's Bluebook
Poor's Register of Directors and Executives
Standard & Poor's publications
Thomas's Register of American Manufacturers
Annual reports
For public companies, documents required to be filed with the Securities Exchange Commission, such as registration statements and the annual report form (10-K).

Many of the above can be found at your local public library. Placement offices should also have other printed material on companies that recruit at their school.

Stock brokers may know something about the company and its personnel. College professors who teach subjects in the field of the company's line of work may be helpful. You can contact the company's public relations department and get quite a bit of information about the company. If you know someone who works there, or know someone who can introduce you to someone who works there, you can get first-hand insider information.

Reader Walter S. Keller, Jr., suggests another way to get information:

> Instead of anonymously contacting the company's public relations department, I have stated to them I'm expecting to be interviewed shortly. This allows them to be more specific in selecting literature to give me. I've done this by phone and in person, walking in and being directed to public relations by the receptionist.
>
> Perhaps the biggest bonus of this approach is that they usually give me copies of the company's house organ. From these I have

gleaned such nuggets as the fact that my interviewer had recently received his Ph.D., that another interviewer was a new father of twins, and in one case that the department I was interested in was initiating several major programs.

A less traditional avenue is to find the cocktail lounge near the company's offices where the workers go after work and drop in for a drink at quitting time. If you can strike up a conversation with one of the company's employees this can help you gather data in preparation for your interview and give you a valuable insight into the company and its morale. It can help you to make a judgment on the company and determine how happy you would be working in such an environment.

If your interview has been arranged by an executive search firm or a placement agency, you can probe the search consultant for information. The consultant will have already done a preliminary check on you and will probably have held an interview to prescreen you. She is placing her reputation on the line by recommending you for an interview, so she wants you to look as good as possible. Ask her as many questions as you want about the company and the person who will be interviewing you. The consultant should brief you thoroughly. You are money to her. If her client offers you a job and you accept it, she gets a big fee, so she's trying her best to make a marriage.

What information do you want on the company? First, of course, you want to know what it does. Is it a conglomerate? What areas is it in? What does it manufacture? What does it sell? If it performs services, what services? Is its profit trend up or down? Is it expanding or contracting? What are its prospects?

You will also want to know about the area where the open job is. The same questions you ask about the company can be asked about the division in which you may be working.

Learn about the product

If there's a product involved, learn about the product. When I first took a job as a young attorney for Litton Industries,

I was interviewing for the position as an assistant division counsel for their Guidance & Control Systems Division. That name alone was enough to boggle my mind. A scientist I was not. After a little research, I found that they made something called an inertial navigation system. That was worse than the name of the division. What was an inertial navigation system?

Finally I went to a fraternity brother who had majored in engineering and asked him if he knew what it was all about. He explained to me that inertial navigation was a method of navigating whereby the system allows you, if you know your starting point, to measure speed and distance and therefore know where you are at all times. He also explained the components of the system.

When I went into my interview with the division counsel, I astounded him by my ability to speak the jargon of inertial navigation. Of course I didn't completely understand it then, nor do I now, but I exhibited at least a modicum of intelligence about the subject.

He later told me that I was the first person he had interviewed for the job who knew anything about inertial navigation. Since he didn't understand it any better than I did, his being relieved of this obligation was a big plus in my favor. He also said he knew it must have been difficult to understand it well enough to have the confidence to discuss it. My initiative in going to this extent to prepare for the interview impressed him.

So few people have the interest or drive to do this amount of work preparing for an interview. If you do, you should have a big advantage over your competition.

Find out about the interviewer

You should discover as much as you can about the person who will be conducting the interview. Where was she born? Where was she educated? What's she done that's unusual? What's her area of expertise?

If you know the name of your interviewer, you can make discreet inquiries about her by dropping her name. This can be a dangerous tack, however, because it could get back to her. Asking someone, "Do you know Jackie Spratt?" can elicit affirmative responses. If it does, however, you don't want the person with whom you're speaking to go to Spratt and mention that you were asking about her—so make it clear that you don't know her personally.

This technique is offered with the disclaimer that if the interviewer discovers that you were doing a background check on her, she may be offended. No one likes to have someone probing about them, even if your intentions are all the best. So if you are inclined to go to this much trouble, be aware that it could backfire and ruin your interview before you walk in the door. If you're not excited by James Bond snooping in someone's file drawers in the dim of night with a flashlight and footsteps coming down the hall, this may not be for you.

An interviewer sometimes will try to get inside you, perhaps by asking you questions involving some controversy. While most often these questions are asked to determine your thought patterns rather than your positions on issues, if you have a general feel for the interviewer, it can save you from voicing a dogmatic opinion that would offend her and result in your rejection. If the interviewer is Jewish, you may decide to play down your admiration for Yasser Arafat. If she is an active member of the local American Civil Liberties Union, you may not want to emphasize your support of preventive detention.

If you can learn something about the person who is going to interview you, you can steer clear of sensitive areas and concentrate on discussing things that you may have in common.

If you know something about the interviewer, you are better able to affect the flow of the interview and keep on topics where you won't offend. You may even get her to depart from the relatively impersonal format of a selection interview and discuss more personal matters. In order to receive an offer, an interviewee wants to have the interviewer come out of the interview with the feeling, "I really liked that person."

Beware of the generation gap! If there's a big difference between your age and the age of your interviewer, you can leave an extremely negative impression if you use words with which she is unfamiliar or that emphasize the disparity in your eras. This is especially true if you are much younger than your interviewer. While an older interviewee might not turn a younger interviewer off by using "23 skiddoo" or "bad trip," a young interviewee risks instant oblivion by the involuntary use of jargon like "bogus" or "yo, chill out" that's sweeping the campuses and clubs but hasn't reached the ears of an interviewer who goes home from work each night to dinner and bed. For example, if your interviewer makes a good point, you'd do well to stifle your impulse to compliment her by saying, "Awesome, dude!" Your contemporaries might appreciate such a comment. Your interviewer probably won't.

Reader Jennifer Ruggaber of Syracuse, New York, advises care in the use of vernacular when she writes:

> If you're just out of college, beware of the slang words you use when conversing. Often you don't even realize you're using them, but they won't be overlooked by older people who are unfamiliar with current slang. They may even conclude that you are immature and inarticulate.
>
> First, pinpoint these words, then think of (or make a list of) synonymous and more descriptive words that could be substituted. Next, *practice* using them *before* the interview. You'll feel more relaxed during the interview if these words come naturally.

There is one colloquialism (and I use the term advisedly) that is almost certain to turn off any interviewer with even a passing allegiance to proper grammar. While most idiomatic language is fairly harmless, sometimes something sneaks into usage through the back door that is horribly offensive to anyone not familiar with it. If you want to get off on the wrong foot in an interview quickly, use "I go" or "she goes" in lieu of "I said" or "she said." Maybe on the campus or in your dorm you can get away with substituting "go" for "said," but definitely not in the interview. This has become so commonplace among young adults that many use it as a matter of course. If you do, you should adopt Jennifer Ruggaber's advice and work diligently to erase it from your involuntary memory, at least while you're going through interviews.

Often it's the small things like the use of an offensive idiom that can spell the difference between success or failure in an interview. Maybe your interviewer never misses "Saturday Night Live" and will take an immediate liking to you if you use "no way, yes way." But you take a big risk in pinning your hopes on this eventuality. It's better to play it safe and avoid current slang.

There is a flip side to this advice, however. If you use current slang among your contemporaries just to fit in, and can live happily without ever speaking it again, then you should eschew it in the interview. If, on the other hand, slang is a part of your personality, then avoiding it might not be the wise thing to do. If you speak like Henry Higgins in the interview, only to revert to your idiomatic Eliza Doolittle language when you start working, they'll realize they didn't hire the person they thought they hired and the job might not last very long. Further, if you are comfortable with the way you speak, and the people for and with whom you work find it offensive, you might not be very happy in the job yourself. So if speaking slang is part of you, then using it in the interview is okay. If the interviewer doesn't like it, you've still done a good interview because you won't get an offer for a job in which you wouldn't have been content anyway.

Don't flaunt your preparation

Many interviewees make the mistake of flaunting their preparation in the interview. They want to make sure that the interviewer is aware of the fact that they had so much interest in the job that they devoted a lot of time to researching and preparing for the interview. This can come across as insincere. The reason that you do the preparation is to make yourself ready for the interview by learning about the company and the person conducting the interview. But you want this information so that you can make an intelligent decision. If you did the preparation only to impress the interviewer with your knowledge and she perceives this, it will be a negative factor.

Interviewers can spot interviewees who are acting in a "programmed" manner, rather than naturally. If the interviewer feels that the interviewee is playing a game with the interview, it will rapidly turn from a selection interview into a rejection interview.

If you've done your research and preparation, it'll come across to the interviewer in the natural course of the interview. You will convey possession of knowledge and information through your demeanor and reactions to questions. If it comes across naturally, the reaction will be positive.

Prepare your own questions

You can almost surely count on being asked, sometime in the course of every interview, if you have any questions of your own to ask, and it pays to prepare ahead of time for this. Reader Lisa F. Dawkings of Englewood, Colorado, describes the consequences of failing to do so:

> I know it's a good idea to ask questions, but what does one ask when the interviewer has answered all possible questions before he asks if I have any? Often those interviews are more of a monologue (on the interviewer's part) than a dialogue, and I feel I came off as something short of bright when I have nothing to ask.

Here are some suggestions from reader John Meyers of Richmond, Virginia:

1. Who would I be working for?
2. May I have a company organization chart?
3. Tell me about your company.
4. What do you look for in a candidate for this position?
5. How many candidates are you interviewing for this position?
6. How would you describe this position?
7. Where would I be working?
8. Does your company have other locations?
9. How is the work divided between locations?
10. How many hours per week do you expect me to work?

11. What do you pay for overtime?

12. Do you reimburse employees for moving expenses?

If your interviewer has answered all of the questions you have plus all of these, and your interviewer is as talkative as Ms. Dawkins's interviewer, probably something will have occurred to you that you'd like to know about her. If not, and if she has answered all your questions about the job, ask the interviewer how *she* likes working for the company and if there's anything she doesn't like about it. That's a good question any interviewee should be prepared to ask because it can elicit information about the company you won't be able to get elsewhere and it might catch your interviewer by surprise.

If you have done the preparation of looking into yourself recommended in this book, you should have developed enough insight into yourself to have many questions about what you will want in a company for which you work. This preparation will allow you to develop a list of questions that are important to you. The questions I list here merely comprise the tip of the iceberg to get you started. (For further help on this, see Appendix D.)

Don't make the mistake of asking questions for the sake of the question itself. Whittaker's Joseph Alibrandi says, "Many times guys will ask questions because they think it's intelligent and it satisfies some requirement that somebody set up for the kinds of things you should know about a company. When somebody asks a question like that, I think that he's asking for my benefit. If that was really important to him he could have found out by looking at the annual report. It gives you a feel for the kind of person he is. You feel that he can't separate the cosmetics from the fundamentals. I'm amazed that he's sitting with me and really believes that that cosmetic is going to help him. It would be a real negative because what you're really looking for are the basic traits, honesty, ability to work with people, ability to relate to people."

Ernest Hemingway developed a way of writing in which he would write a story and then omit several pages at the beginning, theorizing that something omitted can affect the reader as if it were there. He used this method in several short stories and in his first novel, *The Sun Also Rises*. This same theory applies to an interviewee's preparation. Even though you do not discuss all you know about the company and the person conducting the interview, you will convey a sense of knowledge during the interview. Knowledge obtained through preparation, even though unstated, will have a presence and will affect the interview and the feeling developed by the interviewer.

Just as a person with power doesn't have to say, "I am powerful," you don't have to say, "I know a lot about you and your company." The powerful person radiates power. The knowledgeable person radiates knowledge. To discuss it, to bring it out in the open for no reason, is to diminish it and to turn a plus to a negative.

CHECKLIST

★ Preparation is the key to achievement.
★ Don't go into the interview thinking that the interviewer knows exactly what she wants out of the interview and will ask the appropriate questions.
★ Write your autobiography.
★ Make a list of what things in a job will make you happy.
★ Make a list of the things in a job that you don't like.
★ Separate the list of what you like into requirements versus desires.
★ Ensure that your thinking is logical when you deal with your requirements.
★ Learn as much as you can about the company you're interviewing.
★ Interviewers want to know specifically why you are interested in their company.
★ One question to expect is, "What can you add to our company as an employee?"
★ Learn about the product or service the company manufactures, sells, or performs.

Preparation

★ Learn about the interviewer.

★ Prepare your own list of questions to ask.

★ Don't ask questions for the sake of impressing your interviewer with the question itself.

★ Don't flaunt your preparation.

TYPES OF INTERVIEWS

The word *interview* is derived from the French, *entrevoir*, ("to see one another, meet"). Although the term generally applies to job applicants (for instance, Webster's defines it as "a formal consultation usually to evaluate qualifications [as of a prospective student or employee]), it should not be so limited. An interview includes any confrontation between two people when the understood purpose is for at least one of the two to make an evaluation of the other **for any reason.**

There are two basic types of interview—the screening interview and the selection interview or interview for hire. Screening interviews are generally conducted by a staff member in the personnel department who may have had formal training in interview methodology. Selection interviews are conducted by the supervisor or manager to whom the open position reports. In large organizations you may have to go through both a screening interview and a selection interview. For very high level jobs, applicants often go through a series of screening and selection interviews.

Screening interviews

The screening interviewer's goal is very simple: to send a qualified candidate to the supervisor who is requesting an employee. Therefore he is looking for a candidate with a solid background and will ask questions relating to work experience. (In this chapter we'll assume the interviewer is a man.) He will probe for areas of inconsistency in your résumé and will try to find out if you have lied on your résumé or in your responses. What kind of personality you have will be of little importance.

The screening interviewer has generally been trained in interview methodology. He follows the rules and formats in which he has been trained and probably has digested most of the theories set forth in books on how to interview.

Sharyn Cole, who was director of placement and in charge of hiring the entire staff of the giant Los Angeles Bonaventure Hotel when it first opened, says, "The screening interview is a process of elimination. You try to weed out unacceptable candidates."

John Munro Fraser, in the *The Handbook of Employment Interviewing*, sets forth the view of the personnel function in conducting an interview: "We must get at the facts of a candidate's previous history; and we must go into it as thoroughly and in as great detail as is possible in the time available . . . . It is upon facts alone that a sound assessment can be established."

For the interviewer, the purpose of a good screening interview is to get facts. Since your purpose is to get past the screener to the selection interview, when you recognize a screening interview, you may put it to your benefit by providing the interviewer with the facts he so fervently desires.

In the screening interview, there is very little personal involvement on the part of the screener, who will probably never see the candidate again after the interview. He needn't worry about how you will get along with other people, because he will not have to work with you. Further, he will not be subject to criticism on the point of personality because it's not part of what he's looking for. His motivation is a relatively negative one: not to make a mistake in evaluating the facts for which he can be criticized. For example, if a candidate for executive secretary was sent to an executive and it was discovered that the candidate didn't know how to type, the screener would be vulnerable to reproach. If it was found that the candidate typed 100 words per minute, but had a terrible personality and alienated the executive, the screener would not be subject to criticism at all. The responsibility was not to make personality assessments but to analyze the factual data and determine whether the candidate had the skills and experience to qualify for the position. Therefore the screener is very careful that his judgments are backed up by cold, hard facts. Since he does not have the power to make the hire decision, his intuitive feeling about the candidate is irrelevant.

The screening interviewer may know very little about the job for which the candidate is interviewing or about the supervisor to whom the candidate will report if hired. He works in a vacuum. He receives a requisition for a position with bare outline requirements. What does he do? He matches facts with facts. The purpose of this interview is simply to verify facts on the résumé and to endeavor to elicit more facts.

Uppermost in the screener's mind is not to find the best person for the position, not to make a judgment on the candidate's personality, not to determine the candidate's thought processes; it is to ensure that the person interviewed has the qualifications in terms of education and experience for the position.

What is written here is not intended to be critical of the screening function. The job is a difficult one. But you must recognize that a screener is just that, a screener. The function a screener performs is valuable because it saves the supervisor precious time in interviewing and rejecting obviously unqualified candidates.

If you survive the screening interview, it is generally an indication that your qualifications for the position are acceptable as far as the facts are concerned: you have enough experience and there is nothing on your résumé or in your background to disqualify you (such as a record of convictions of crime or unexplained terminations from prior employment).

The screening interview is mostly a clerical function, consisting of checking the facts on the résumé, and filling in gaps in time that may appear on the résumé.

A serious personality conflict that emerges during a screening interview could result in rejection at this stage, but it is something that would occur only if you brought about the problem, since the interviewer is not probing in this area.

Knowing this going into the interview, you should conduct yourself accordingly. You should give the interviewer the facts for which he is searching. You should be pleasant and avoid controversy. Above all, avoid volunteering facts for which the interviewer is not searching.

The screening interviewer is an expert at discovering reasons not to send you on to the next stage, the selection interview. **The screener may not have the power to hire you, but does have the power to reject you,** and will do so if you appear unqualified in any way. Therefore, in the screening interview, the key is to follow the interviewer's lead. Do not try to exert any control over the interview. Answer any questions asked in a simple, straightforward manner and leave it at that. Since you have nothing to gain, don't put yourself in a position from which you can only maintain the status quo or lose.

Selection interviews

The supervisor who is interviewing a potential employee has totally different motivations from the screener. As we have seen, the screener's primary concern is to avoid criticism by weeding out unacceptable candidates. The supervisor's problem is much more complex. If the supervisor hires someone who doesn't work out and has to be let go, the mistake is likely to cost the company thousands of dollars.

A new employee naturally has to go through a period of orientation before becoming totally productive. Still, the employee has to be paid, so the company is not getting its money's worth in work product during this break-in period. But it is making an investment in the future. If the employee has to be fired, the future will no longer be a factor. That investment is down the drain. It has been estimated that a bad hiring decision by a top manager costs $60,000, a middle manager $25,000, and a lower-middle manager $7,500. That's what companies figure it costs them to train someone. Not only is that money gone forever, but the time lost is an additional expense to the company because the hiring procedure must begin anew.

So, the supervisor isn't just worried about getting stuck with an undesirable worker. There are very real financial and organizational pressures to contend with.

Very few supervisors are experienced in conducting interviews. Most books on personnel interviewing are only read by those who conduct screening interviews. Although they are directed toward supervisors as well as personnel people, the supervisor who has read even one book of this sort is as rare as a sailboat in the Sahara. A supervisor's job is not to interview but to perform a certain function (such as manufacturing a widget or selling that widget or keeping the books of the company). So job-related reading will deal with the manufacturing processes or the techniques of selling or how to make debits and credits. As important as interviewing technique may be to the portion of his job that pertains to hiring and managing people, he doesn't think about how to interview until he is faced with the situation. When that occurs, he simply conducts it using his intuition, hoping to get it over with in as short a time as possible.

Knowing this, you will want to approach the selection interview in a much different manner than you would the screening interview. Instead of being bland and brief and sticking to facts, when you find yourself in the same room with the person who is going to make the hire/no hire decision, you must assume responsibility for the content of the interview, unless you run into that rare supervisor with interviewing experience as discussed in Chapter 1.

Above all, recognize that you are breaking into his routine. His normal day does not include a selection interview. He's got all the responsibilities of his job on his mind, in addition to trying to find an acceptable employee. Therefore, he is probably completely unprepared for the interview, and he's wondering what he's going to do to make a determination to fill this vacancy, how he's going to do it, and how he can do it in as short a time period as possible.

Despite all the pressures that are placed on selection interviewers to make a good decision, the way they arrive at their judgment is not scientific. You must recognize that no matter what they say they are looking for, they are going to reach their conclusion based upon the feeling they have after the interview about the interviewee. The way you think, the way you express yourself, what you say, how you say it, your manner and style, all are more important to the selection interviewer than the bare facts on your résumé. It is a very **personal** assessment. Each selection interviewer is different; each makes decisions based upon his prejudices.

It is always advisable in any endeavor to approach it as if you are going to be faced with a conscientious, knowledgeable, and well-researched person. If you take this approach, you will never be unpleasantly surprised. If you enter expecting less than the best and you happen to get the best, you'll be at a disadvantage. On the other hand, if you enter expecting the best and get less than the best, you'll have the advantage.

Interview styles

There are certain basic interviewing formats that are commonly used, and it is helpful to know about them ahead of time so that you will be well-prepared under all circumstances:

Directed interview

The directed interview is used by most personnel department interviewers for screening. It follows a definite pattern. The interviewer works from an outline and asks specific questions within a certain time frame. The interviewer has a checklist and makes notations about the candidate's responses. Most professional interviewers use the directed interview. While appropriate and useful for screening, it is of the least value in a selection interview because it is too structured and impersonal to get at the personality of the candidate.

Nondirective interview

The nondirective interview is generally used by nonprofessionals. It has a loosely structured format, one where the interviewee is allowed to talk about any subject desired. The questions are broad and general, and they invite the interviewee to take control. The interviewer acts more like a moderator than anything else. It is an excellent format for bringing out an interviewee's personality. Most nonprofessional interviewers go into interviews with no formal preparation and are not set up to conduct a directed interview so they try to get the interviewee to talk. The result is a semi-nondirective interview.

Stress interview

For the interviewer, the stress interview can be a lot of fun. For the unsuspecting interviewee, it can be sheer hell. The stress interview was developed by the Germans prior to World War II. Initially, and in its classic form, it consisted of taking close-up film of a candidate's face while he was being administered painful electric shocks. This crude technique has been refined over the years, and now it generally consists of long periods of silence, challenging your opinions, seeming to be unfriendly or brusque, and other attitudes directed toward making you uncomfortable.

Most interviews contain a certain amount of stress by their very nature. The introduction of intentional stress will be something that you will notice if you are alert. For example, you are answering questions and suddenly the interviewer lapses into silence and stares at you introducing stress into the interview to see how you'll react. If you fidget or start tapping your fingers or look down at your shoes, your actions tell something—and it's not good from your point of view. If on the other hand, you return the stare pleasantly and expectantly without showing signs of agitation, you've probably passed the test.

It is extremely infrequent that a selection interview is entirely a stress interview. The most effective interview is a combination of the nondirective and the stress types. In the hands of a skillful interviewer, you can be led through a maze of ups and downs, and an amazingly accurate picture of your personality will emerge within thirty minutes.

There are other examples of the introduction of stress into an interview of which you should be aware. The main reason you should know about these techniques is so that you may combat them. And the best way to combat them is to recognize them for what they are. This will give you the advantage because you won't react to what's being done; rather you'll recognize it as stress and just accept it as a normal part of the interview.

For example, one way to introduce stress into an interview that most don't recognize is to keep you waiting long past your appointed hour. Maybe there's a business reason you're being kept waiting. Maybe your interviewer is chronically late. But if you assume that being kept waiting is just a ploy by the interviewer to see how you'll react you will not feel the anger and frustration that is the normal result of being kept waiting. Instead you'll say to yourself, "This person is applying stress!" And you'll just sit there and enjoy knowing that you're handling it beautifully.

Another way for an interviewer to apply stress is to arrange the seating so that you are looking out the window into bright light coming from behind him. The result is that the pupils of your eyes contract, allowing less light into your eyes so that the interviewer may appear as a mere shadow, making it extremely difficult for you to see any expression whatever on his face and almost impossible to see his eyes. This can be extremely disconcerting, but if you recognize it as an intentional scheme used by your interviewer to see how you handle it, you will be able to bear up under the burden much easier than if you are just bothered by the bad lighting and grouse about it in your mind.

Anytime you can recognize a level of discomfort as an intentional stratagem being used by the interviewer to test you, you will be much better able to endure whatever it is. Try to think of everything that happens to you in an interview, no matter how seemingly innocuous or happenstance, as something intentionally imposed upon you by the interviewer as a planned part of the interview. It might not be the case, but this could save you from reacting in such a way as to cost you a successful interview.

Of course, stress may be applied more cruelly. An interviewer for one of the world's largest law firms once asked an African-American female student at the University of Chicago Law School how she would react to being called a "black bitch" or a "nigger" by adversaries or colleagues. Later in the interview she said she enjoyed golf, and the interviewer asked her why African-Americans didn't have their own country clubs, "like Jews."

When the student complained to school officials, the law firm apologized, stating that they "do not condone or tolerate that kind of statement. It was unthinking, and we do not approve of it," adding that the interviewer "is not a racist" and made the comments as a "stress test" for the applicant. (Despite the apology, the firm was banned from recruiting at the law school for one year.)

But you should be prepared for the imposition of stress like this. It's rare that it would be imposed in such an aggressive and offensive manner, but if it is and you can immediately recognize it as a test, even if you are offended, you should be able to handle it calmly. If you get angry, you lose. If you say to yourself, "This is stress, the interviewer really doesn't mean to offend," then you can react in a way that is in your best interest. While there's always the possibility that you are being interviewed by a direct descendant of Genghis Khan, it's in your interest to discard this possibility and act on the assumption that the interviewer is imposing stress on you to see how you will react.

And how to react? There are two possibilities. The first is to answer the question. "How would you react to being called a 'black bitch'?" Tell him. "Why don't blacks have their own golf courses, like Jews?" Answer the question. "I don't know," sounds like a good answer to me, although you could go into how you feel about discriminatory private clubs if you have a feeling about it.

The other possibility is to challenge the interviewer in as professional a tone as possible. You could tell him how you would react in a hypothetical situation. You could also tell him you feel that the question is out of line, if that's the way you feel. However, you should always recognize that the interviewer might have a legitimate reason for asking this type of question and imposing this type of stress. If you're being considered for a position as a litigator, the question could be a legitimate attempt to determine how you would function in the real world because litigation can be like war. So maybe the question was a legitimate imposition of stress to determine what would happen if the situation arose in the real world.

I'm not justifying the offensive imposition of stress here. But you must constantly keep in mind during the interview process that you are looking for a job and that it is not in your best interest to take offense. You should always try to realize that there could be an underlying reason for which a question is asked other than that which is apparent on its face.

If you feel you have been unfairly harassed or discriminated against, you may have recourse under certain federal and state laws. See Chapter 13, Discrimination, for more on this.

Group interview

In a group interview there are many interviewees and either one or several interviewers. This format was originally devised to select officer candidates for the armed forces. Normal one-on-one interviews with résumés and reference checks had not been reliable in determining natural leadership ability. In this method, a group of candidates was assembled and assigned a task to accomplish as a group. The group was then observed during its performance.

It is said that a group will always stratify and that eventually a leader will emerge. Weinland and Gross in their book, *Personnel Interviewing*, say that "this person is apt to be what is called a 'natural leader.' Since he has no credentials, he must win the acceptance of the group and cannot be put in place merely by an external influence."

In a group interview, normal rules no longer hold. You should have a big advantage over other interviewees because the purpose of the group interview is not explained. In a business context, it may be presented as a group discussion. Since you know that the purpose is not to study what is said or the opinions expressed but to determine some characteristics of how you interact with the other members of the group, you should try to determine the characteristics for which the interviewers are searching and direct your attention toward the group with this in mind.

The group interview is rarely used in the United States, but it is a method of which you should be aware in the unlikely event you are faced with it.

Board interview

In a board interview there is one interviewee and many interviewers. A typical board interview is the doctoral candidate's oral examination. The federal government sometimes uses the board interview, too. It is perhaps most common in industry in interviewing for higher-level corporate positions, such as president or vice president.

How you should handle yourself in a board interview does not differ greatly from the normal interview. The only added factor is that there is more than one person, so you cannot concentrate on establishing a rapport with one person. **If you're uneasy, the best way to handle it is to pretend that you are talking to only one person, the one who is questioning you.** In this way you may forget the other eyes that are upon you, and you may, in your mind's eye, convince yourself that you are in a simple one-on-one interview. The two important rules are to be relaxed and to maintain your confidence.

Telephone interviews

Reader More Irvine, a judge on the Board of Industrial Insurance Appeals in Olympia, Washington, writes of a problem people may face when they are looking for work out of their home area:

> I decided to change positions, and I began a job search, mostly with the federal government, and mostly in the Washington, D. C., area. I was able to secure two excellent interviews, one with the U.S. Claims Court and the other with the Appeals Council for the Office of Hearings and Appeals for the Social Security Administration. Because these are federal positions, neither would pay for me to fly out for the interview. The law prohibits it. As a result, I had to make the hard decision of undertaking the expense of flying cross-country or accepting their offer of doing a telephone interview.

Judge Irvine's problem presents a basic economic decision that only the person involved can make. If you can afford to travel to a distant location for an interview, it's an indication of your enthusiasm for the job and your confidence in your ability to get the job. However, if you simply cannot afford it, you should make this fact clear to your interviewer and try for the telephone interview. A telephone interview produces less stress, but it lacks the immediacy of being there in person. If you don't have the funds to finance the trip, then you don't have a choice. If you do have the money but it would impose a hardship, you must make a decision involving several variables:

1. How much do you want the job?
2. Do you know enough about the job to be able to make that kind of decision?
3. How confident are you that, if you spend the money to go to the interview, you'll be offered the job?
4. How will you react if you spend the money to go but don't get an offer?

This problem requires a great deal of self-knowledge and honesty, in addition to an economic decision. Be sure you evaluate it properly and consider all the factors, not just one, because your desire for the job may outweigh the practicalities of the situation. If the interview is a screening interview, it would not seem worth such an expenditure. However, if you've passed the screening stage and the expenditure would be for a selection interview, you should ask for a first-level telephone interview first. In the telephone interview you should be as much interviewer as interviewee, trying to determine as much about the job and the employer as you can. If you then determine that the job's what you want and the person for whom you would be working is acceptable, then you would be in a position to make the difficult decision of whether or not to spend the money for the second interview. You'd have a better feeling for whether you really wanted the job and you'd have a feeling of whether you'd get along with your employer.

Jesse Marvin Unruh Fellowship Program interviews

An excellent example of the combined use of group and board interviews is conducted by the California State Assembly in awarding fellowships for their ten-month fellowship program. Charlotte Ashmun, who has been both an interviewee applying for a fellowship and, subsequently, an interviewer evaluating candidates for fellowships the following year, gives an insider's description of the process from both viewpoints:

It is a four-tiered interviewing system. The first three stages have to do with getting the fellowship itself and the final stage has to do with the placement once you are a Fellow.

First you fill out an application form and there are usually about five hundred applicants for eight fellowships. That's used to screen.

The next stage is a Board Interview that consists of a committee of about nine academic people from throughout the state and Assembly staff who interview you alone. They ask political questions and theoretical questions and quite a range of questions as to how you would deal with problems.

Then the final stage is a Group Interview with the last group of finalists. You go through a process which involves three rooms full of interviewers. The interviewers are divided into three groups also. You go into each of the three rooms in succession and have a discussion on a policy topic.

There's no interference by the interviewers. The entire process is done by the interviewees and their intergroup reactions and that sort of thing.

It's terribly effective, but it's pretty frightening too.

They're looking for how articulate you are, how well you think over a policy issue and they're also looking for people who are going to be abrasive. They're not looking for people who are going to be all talk and no content.

I wasn't impressed with the validity of the test when I went through it. But the next year I participated in it and saw the comparison of the notes by the interviewers and their discussion in choosing who should be selected for the program and who should not. Then I saw that as I stayed with one group all day long and followed them through their process, it became clear quickly who would make it as a Fellow and who would not.

Some people were too shy and would not speak up about their thoughts. In the position that the fellowship holds with the Legislature you're in front of committees and are asked questions about the bills you write by the committee members with the press there and you can't be so shy and retiring that you can't support the bill that you've been working on.

Additionally, a staff member has to be able to stay a staff member and not try to be too much of a star. So although it was good to be able to give some guidance to the group and keep them on track, if you were trying to make yourself look good to the disadvantage of everyone else, that was viewed quite negatively.

Know what the interviewer is looking for

No matter what technique an interviewer uses, each is trying to fill a specific position. A set of specifications will have been formulated for that position, and the interviewer will be looking for certain characteristics.

When the group interview was devised by the armed forces during World War II, it was used to determine the leadership characteristics of the candidates. The interviewers were looking for the person who could take charge of the group naturally. If you knew the purpose, you could gear your performance to that objective.

The California State Assembly's goal is directly contrary. Even though the same format is used—the group interview—the assembly is looking for opposite characteristics: people who will **not** exert their leadership characteristics, people who can function on a staff in an advisory role and leave the leadership to the assembly for whom they will be working.

Once again preparation emerges as of prime importance in determining how to approach an interview. If you know what the interviewer is looking for, you will have a tremendous advantage over the other interviewees because you will be able to key your performance to those characteristics. This knowledge alone may not land you a job offer, but it can protect you against making a gaffe that might result in rejection.

CHECKLIST

★ A screening interviewer is looking just for the facts.
★ A screening interviewer is looking for a reason to reject you rather than a reason to accept you.

★ The purpose of the screening interview is to weed out unacceptable candidates.

★ A screening interviewer is well-trained in the art of interviewing; a selection interviewer generally is not.

★ Don't volunteer anything in a screening interview.

★ Let the screener control both the flow and the content of the interview.

★ Avoid controversy.

★ An interview is a meeting between two people usually for the purpose of evaluating the qualifications or capabilities.

★ Always expect to meet a conscientious, knowledgeable, and well-researched person.

★ A directed interview is structured, impersonal, and generally used only by screening interviewers.

★ A nondirective interview is one where the interviewee is allowed to talk about that which he wishes.

★ A stress interview is designed to make the interviewee uncomfortable and to bring out your insecurities.

★ Most selection interviews are a combination of the nondirective and stress types.

★ A group interview has many interviewees and either one or several interviewers.

★ A board interview uses several interviewers.

★ Try to determine before the interview what the interviewers will be looking for.

★ Be aware of stress. If you are expecting it and recognize it when it is introduced, you will be better able to handle it well by retaining your composure.

ENTHUSIASM

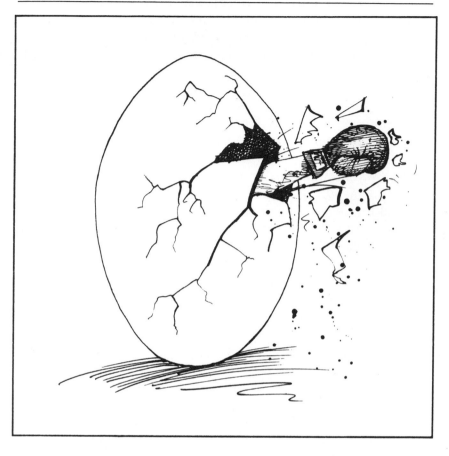

Nothing great has ever been done without enthusiasm.
RALPH WALDO EMERSON

In his book *Successful Salesmanship*, Paul Ivey defines enthusiasm as "a spirit which animates the whole body and makes an attractive and convincing salesman out of an assortment of dead flesh and bones." I'd go a bit further. **Enthusiasm is the exhibition of fervent interest**. And it is highly contagious.

When you take part in an interview, it is not enough just to say you are interested. You must show it through your actions. I've conducted so many interviews in which well-qualified interviewees sit and answer questions as if they are going through some sort of initiation rite. When the interview is over, they just leave, having lost the opportunity to make some positive impression on me. Whether lack of enthusiasm like this is due to fear or nervousness, to the misconception that it is wise to play hard to get, or to just plain ignorance, it is bound to affect the interviewer negatively.

To prevent any such spiraling effect in your own interviews, it is essential that you go into them determined to project a sense of vitality. After all, the interview is an event in itself—something different from an offer or a job. You can be enthusiastic about yourself, your interests, the interests of the interviewer, or the company. The point to remember is that without enthusiasm, you'll risk coming across as a dud.

Reader Raymond L. Berry of Dunsmuir, California, writes:

> About a year ago I moved from the San Francisco Bay Area, where I was a college instructor, to a small town near Mt. Shasta, to help a friend start a small business. I figured with my education and experience I would have no trouble getting a job.
>
> Because I quit my last job, I was not entitled to unemployment benefits, so my savings started to dwindle as I applied for job after job, getting no offers. I made seven different versions of my résumé, left off my education, lowered my expectations, and started applying for minimum wage positions.
>
> Because there is no economic base up here except tourism, jobs are at a premium. But the most frustrating part of this experience is that I was being rejected for the following two reasons.
>
> 1. Employers didn't think I had a valid reason to be up here.
> 2. The eight miles to the next town was considered "too far to go" and I was rejected there because they wouldn't hire anyone from "that town." Part of it I think is small town rivalry, and part because in winter it snows and locals don't think that anyone else knows how to get around.
>
> After reading *Sweaty Palms* I knew I had to change my strategy if I wanted to work, so I threw out my résumé, got rid of my negative attitude, and just used enthusiasm and friendliness. I had three interviews and three job offers. Not career positions, but at least I broke the "no job" syndrome. First time I had an experience like this, and am finding out now that it happens to a lot of others who leave the big city for the mountains. Hope this will be helpful to others who find themselves in similar circumstances.

Treat the interview as an experience

Each interview will probably present you with a different challenge. It's exciting to go into an interview knowing that you'll be presented with the challenge of interpreting the interviewer's personality (and for this chapter, let's assume the interviewer is a man). Maybe you'll need to discover his interests. Maybe you'll need to talk about yourself and your own interests to find a common ground. Even though you can expect similar things from each interview, the challenge is that each interview is unknown from the point of the personality of the interviewer. If you view it this way, you can retain your enthusiasm for each interview.

This doesn't mean you have to prostrate yourself in front of your interviewer, begging for a job about which you know nothing in order to be enthusiastic about an interview. I've had many interviews in which I found out early that the interviewee was not appropriate for the job, but I was so interested in finding out more about him or her that my enthusiasm was unbounded.

Once I interviewed a law student who was interested in working only where he could use his proficiency in the Mandarin dialect of the Chinese language. It was obvious to both of us that the interview would not result in a job offer for him. But he was so enthusiastic about his training in Chinese and his work in Panmunjom, Korea, that it resulted in one of the longest interviews I've ever had. He was enthusiastic about telling me about his interests, and I was enthusiastic to learn more about him. As a result, even though the goal each of us sought, a job offer, was not achieved, this interview stands out as one of the most memorable ones I've ever had, and it was solely because of his enthusiasm. I have recommended him to a couple of corporations that had international departments, and I still keep him in mind years later.

One of the best ways to project enthusiasm is to try to make the other person enthusiastic. Years ago, I read Dale Carnegie's *How to Win Friends and Influence People*. In it he tells how to get people to like you. One of the methods he suggests is to get them to talk about themselves. He tells of picking out some small thing you notice about someone and asking about it. He gives examples, as I do here, of the way this has worked for him and others in the past.

I read his book with a somewhat jaundiced eye, assuming that the examples were there just to fit the rule he was laying down. I didn't think much about it until one day I was sitting in a barber's chair. I had never visited this shop before so I didn't know the barber. Worse, he was extremely taciturn. So I sat in an uncomfortable silence as he cut my hair, responding to my few attempts at conversation with grumbles.

Then I remembered Dale Carnegie. I tried to discover something about the barber and his shop upon which I could comment to see if Carnegie's method could really work. Finally the barber lathered my neck and, after stropping his straight razor, he started shaving my neck. I commented, "Gee, that sure is a sharp razor."

That simple comment was akin to "open sesame." He told me that his father had given him that razor, that it had come from Germany, and that he had used it for years. "There's not another razor like this in America," he said. He was as proud of that razor as a parent of a child. He talked and talked and talked about his razor. I was interested, not only because his story of the razor was unique, but because my innocent remark had opened a door to the man's heart.

No longer withdrawn, he was warm and friendly. I was excited because I had never dreamed that the rules that I had read in Carnegie's book would work so well. I stayed after he had finished my haircut and talked with him for fifteen minutes while he worked on the next man. When I left, he said he hoped I'd come back because he "really enjoyed talking to me," even though all I had done was to ask a question or two while he monopolized the conversation.

I had turned a silently morose barber into a William Jennings Bryan of fire and brimstone just by asking him about his razor. This was the love of his life, apparently, and he was enthusiastic about it. His enthusiasm was contagious. It made me enthusiastic just to listen to him. Although I had little interest in his razor, his tremendous emotion conveyed itself to me and I was caught up in his enthusiasm.

My barber story is not the exception that proves a converse rule. I am constantly amazed at how often it works to bring people out of themselves. When I was practicing law in London, I used the Middle Temple law library to do my research. The American section was on the top floor, and there was rarely anyone else in there but me and the librarian, a wizened old fellow who never opened his mouth or acknowledged my presence.

One day, after months of coming and going, I noticed him reading a book on gardening. Although I'm no expert, I was raised in a house that had a large garden, and one of our flowers was the hibiscus. I stopped by his desk and asked if there were hibiscus in London. He opened like a blooming flower, told me of his garden in Cornwall, the flowers in it, and the years he had devoted to it. From that point on we were bosom buddies.

When you've successfully brought someone out of themselves in this way, you'll be amazed at the rewarding feeling you'll have. I doubt if there's anything I'd rather talk about less than gardening, but I was never bored by the librarian's discussions. The combination of his enthusiasm and the success of my ploy worked to keep my interest aroused.

It's not enough simply to ask a question. You have to project genuine interest. And if you get a response like I did from the barber and the librarian, you're going to be interested. It won't matter if he's talking about the time and methods he uses to observe grass growing; if he's turned on about the subject, you're going to be spellbound, if not by the subject, certainly by the emotion you have sparked.

Be willing to take a chance

Even if it appears that you don't have a chance in a million of landing a particular job, you should still go into the interview with a positive attitude. My files are full of stories of job-seekers who did a little extra, took a chance, and accomplished the seemingly impossible.

When I was in law school, it seemed that 90 percent of my class was interested in practicing international law. On the day when one of the largest international law firms on Wall Street visited campus to interview, the line to sign up was almost unending.

The interviewer was the senior partner in the firm. He also taught a seminar on international law at the law school. He interviewed for three days but made only one offer and that to one of the top students in the class. I was in the seminar he taught, along with another member of the class who had interviewed but been rejected and whose grades caused him to languish in the middle of class. This student was determined he was going to work for that firm and so he was always well prepared for the seminar. Unfortunately the seminar was conducted by associates in the firm, not the partner. Nevertheless, my classmate continued to prepare while the rest of us took it easy, knowing that our grade did not depend on performance in the seminar. One day the associate who was scheduled to appear could not make it, and the senior partner had to conduct the seminar—but he wasn't prepared at all. He was saved by my classmate, who virtually took over the class that evening. He was the only one who was prepared, and he talked for almost the entire two hours. The senior partner was so impressed that he offered the student a job and, in storybook fashion, the student is now a partner in the firm.

By showing enthusiasm and ingenuity and perseverance he impressed the one who had to make the decision. The job was offered not so much because of the interviewee's quality but because of the extra effort he took to figure out how to get the job after the initial rejection. This way of thinking will impress an interviewer time and again. So do something unusual to set you apart from the others. Be enthusiastic.

As a teenager, Eddie Rickenbacker wanted desperately to work for the Frayer Miller automobile manufacturers, so he started hanging around the plant on his days off. Finally Lee Frayer noticed him and asked him why he was always hanging around every Sunday. Rickenbacker told him that he wanted a job. Frayer said that they didn't have anything he could do. But Rickenbacker had noticed how dirty the place was and told Frayer that there was something he could do and he'd be back the next Sunday.

He arrived at 7 a.m. "with broom and brush" and worked feverishly. When Frayer arrived at 8:30, half the work area was spotless and the other half filthy. Frayer smiled and said that Rickenbacker had his job.

Reader Margot L. Wawra of Clearbrook, British Columbia, tells of two instances in which her enthusiasm paid off:

> When I came to Canada thirty-five years ago my knowledge of English was limited. So I went to the university of our town, sitting in free lectures where I could and devouring books and magazines in the library. One day I noticed on the blackboard a job opportunity for a library helper. I applied. The interviewing woman looked at my neat portfolio and my past experiences and remarked that I seemed well qualified but she was afraid that my knowledge of English was not yet sufficient. That didn't dampen my enthusiasm: "I will work the first month without pay, then you can see what I can do." Instead they hired me but at the lowest possible wages. I didn't mind. I worked there for a couple of years and then entered the university as an art student. I made my B.A. with great honors and did postgraduate work in Los Angeles. Then I opened an art studio in our town where I worked on my sculptures and paintings and taught art classes.
>
> Years down the road, our local YWCA needed a program director. The salary was very tempting, and with two degrees in my pocket, I felt confident. The executive director seemed very interested, though she probed in all directions, and I sensed a hidden agenda, a hesitation in her voice in connection with certain questions. I tuned in on her wavelength and heard myself say: "I am very interested in the work, even if there is no prospect of long-range employment. If you decide to hire me, I plan to keep my art studio open. I like to spend my spare time there and then I can slip back into teaching whenever my work here ends." The director showed signs of relief. She had been afraid to carry a highly paid employee longer than needed. I got the position and worked for the Y for many happy years.

These stories point up the fact that sometimes you have to take a gamble. To do so you must be so enthusiastic about the potential rewards that you are willing to risk what prospectively looks like certain failure. Without enthusiasm, your frame of mind will tell you that your actions are illogical and a waste of time. With enthusiasm your frame of mind is such that you will not admit failure, and you will then proceed with abandon.

Attitude

Because you radiate what you feel, your state of mind will be directly related to the success or failure of your interview. If your attitude is bad, there's no way that you can be enthusiastic. If you enter the interview with a chip on your shoulder, you'll be written off in a trice.

I conducted an interview at a law school several years ago that epitomizes how a bad attitude can affect an interviewee's enthusiasm. The interviewee showed up dressed as if he were going to play football in the mud. He wore a dirty sweatshirt with holes in it, dirty blue jeans, and old Adidas sneakers. Although he had an excellent scholastic record, he responded to my questions sullenly and abrasively. Finally, after the videotaping was over, I asked him if he showed up for all his interviews dressed that way.

This was what he was waiting for. All the rancor in him exploded. "If they don't like the way I look, the hell with 'em."

This fellow was so proud of his anti-establishment posture that it dominated his personality. His antagonism for the way people dressed permeated the interview. Lighted bamboo shoots under his fingernails couldn't have affected his interview worse.

His goal in the interview was to make the point that he would do, speak, and dress as he pleased and no one was going to change him. He knew in advance that his dress was atypical for an interview and that it would be noticed. He waited during the entire interview for me to bring it up, and when he got his chance, he exploded.

He sat through the entire interview waiting for a fight. He flaunted his sloppy attire like a flung gauntlet. The content of the interview was merely a prelude for making his point. Even had the subject not been raised, he would have blown the interview because he came across as sullen and negative.

More often, however, the problem with attitude is not a childish temperament but a defeatist outlook. If you have been through a few interviews and have not received any offers or encouragement, it's very easy to become downcast and feel that you're a chronic failure. You must do everything in your power to overcome this mindset because, while a sense of failure or doom may not make much difference in simple social contact, in an interview it can easily cause you to fail. An interviewer is trying to get at the person beneath the surface. The worst thing that you can display is a sense of gloom or defeat. If you do not believe in yourself, why should the interviewer?

No matter how many rejections you may receive, you must keep your outlook bright and positive.

The most an author can do is to offer his advice and ideas. It is up to the reader to decide whether to accept the advice and then to decide whether to use it. You may read this book, find it entertaining, and even believe it. But if you don't try the things outlined here, it will be to no avail. **I urge you to lose your inhibitions and give the techniques a whirl.** I'm sure you will find that you'll get far more out of an interview, are less nervous going in, and more confident during the interview. You should find that your interviews will flow more easily and that you will establish a better rapport with your interviewer. Best of all, whether you get a job offer or not, you'll come out of each interview feeling that you have learned something new.

CHECKLIST

★ You must show that you are interested.

★ Communicate your interest to the interviewer.

★ Be interested in the interview as an event in itself.

★ Lose your inhibitions and try what you've learned.

★ Enthusiasm begins with a positive attitude.

★ Think that you're going to win.

★ Make an impression on the one who is to make the decision.

★ Be willing to gamble on what may logically appear to be certain failure.

QUESTION AND ANSWER

No matter how many questions you may ask of the interviewer (for this chapter let's assume the interviewer is a man and the interviewee is a woman), and no matter how much control you are able to assert over the interview, the essence of any interview remains locked into the format of a question-and-answer session run by the interviewer. Ultimately, whether your interview will be successful or not will depend on your ability to answer the interviewer's questions effectively.

To do this, you will want to prepare yourself by doing research on the interviewer, the company, and the job for which you are applying as discussed in Chapter 2. You should also review the list of typical interview questions

(see Appendix A). If any of these questions give you difficulties, work out an answer so that you'll be ready if you're
hit with it in an interview. Remember the old saying, "To be
forewarned is to be forearmed."

It's important to understand, however, that in the
question-and-answer session, the interviewer is trying to do
more than find out if you are qualified for the position. The
interviewer is also trying to find out what kind of person
you are, and this subjective feeling is apt to be the most
important aspect of the interview.

In the appendices you will find lists of commonly asked
questions. This book will not provide you with canned responses to these, or any other questions you might be asked
in an interview. The purpose of an interview is for the interviewer and the interviewee to get to know one another.
That purpose is not accomplished by the interviewee using
my words to answer questions.

What this book will give you is the confidence to answer
any question you might be asked and to answer it yourself in your own words from your own experience. After
you finish reading *Sweaty Palms*, you'll be able to enter any
interview without the fear of being surprised by what's going to happen. If you take the advice to heart, you'll know
yourself well enough to be able to handle anything an interviewer might throw at you. Anybody who gives you
canned answers to prospective questions is doing you a dis-
service. Not only will it impede your growth as a person
and rob you of the confidence and pride you should have
in yourself, but an interviewer who hears the same answer
more than once will immediately realize what has happened
and that will not result in his forming a favorable impression.

The questions and answers of an interview are merely the tools
used to make an evaluation, the trees in the forest of impression. The
manner in which you answer the questions and whether or not you
appear self-confident are far more important than the words you use
in your answer. Your goal, then, is to use the format of the inter-
view to establish the proper rapport with the interviewer and gener-
ate a positive feeling. How the interviewer feels about you will have
greater weight than your qualifications when it comes to making final
judgments.

When the Beatles were still struggling Liverpool musicians, their manager, Brian Epstein, had tried for months to get them a tryout with a record company. Finally he convinced producer George Martin to give them an audition. Martin was favorably impressed, and the rest is history. But what was it that persuaded Martin to give the greatest songsters of the generation their start? In a candid interview, Martin said, "It wasn't their music that sold them to me; it was their charm. They were very charming people."

When you realize that the Beatles got their first record contract on the basis of charm rather than musical ability, you will understand the importance of making a good impression. Martin's admission should be enshrined in every interviewee's mind, and should be recalled before the start of each interview.

There's a distinction to be made between preparing answers to questions and preparing to answer questions, and this distinction can mean the difference between a successful interview and an unsuccessful one. The purpose of this chapter is to give advice on how to handle questions in a manner calculated to leave a good impression on the interviewer. Remember, one of your prime goals in any interview is to enhance the feeling the interviewer develops about you. It's not only the content of your answers that contribute to this feeling. The *manner* in which you answer them is as important as what you say.

Listen to the question

The first mistake that many interviewees make is that they don't listen to the question. In order to avoid misunderstandings, or giving answers that miss the point of the question, always listen very carefully to the question and the way it is phrased. If the interviewer asks for specific information, don't play semantic games; answer the question specifically. If you don't wish to answer, sometimes it's better to decline frankly than to beat around the bush with an evasive reply. Later we'll discuss when ignoring this rule might be in your best interest.

The ambiguous question

One of the reasons answers often do not address the questions is that interviewees tend to make assumptions and then base their answers on these assumptions without stating them.

In their book *Pairing,* George Bach and Ronald Deutsch warn never to "assume or predict that you know what your partner is thinking until you have checked out the assumption in plain language; nor assume or predict how he will react, what he will accept or reject." This is easy to say but very difficult to do, particularly in an interview. You can't state your assumptions prior to answering a question as if you were writing a legal brief. People are not machines, and they don't converse like machines.

While psychological self-help books like *Pairing* treat things on a plane where all solutions are ideal and people react consistently, in reality this is not true. Each person is different from another, and each reacts differently. So while the scenarios that are acted out in these books always work out the way the authors intend, their successful conclusions may bear little correlation to real life.

If a question could be interpreted in more than one way, and you are unsure about the point, ask for a clarification. For example, one question that is often asked in interviews is "What are your goals?" This is ambiguous; people generally have several types of goals—personal, recreational, professional. When I ask this question, I am as interested in the content of the reply, as I am in how the interviewee handles the inherent ambiguity of the question. Will the answer be, "Well, I want to be happy and raise a nice family," or "I want to be manager of the department," or "I've always wanted to break ninety on the golf course"? Or will there be a request for clarification? How the interviewee interprets the question, the assumptions she makes, tells me something as valuable about her as the actual content of the answer.

Often the answer will be a request for a clarification. "What do you mean? Do you want to know what my professional goals are or what I want out of life?" There is nothing wrong with this answer. It is quite good. I then choose what

I want to hear, and the interviewee answers accordingly. This type of answer involves no risk. There is a question in the interviewee's mind and rather than guess at the interviewer's meaning, she clarifies the ambiguity and then answers based upon the clarification by the interviewer.

When a question is ambiguous, the ball is in your court. You can do with it what you want. If there's something you want to bring out during the interview, and the ambiguous question gives you the opportunity to say what you want, don't ask for the clarification. Interpret the question the way you wish and answer it to your best advantage. If, on the other hand, the ambiguity troubles you, and it does not give you a waited-for opportunity, ask for the clarification. There is no risk involved. You find out what the interviewer wants to know, and supply the information.

The thinking pause

Another technique you may use in answering questions is to think over an answer before you give it, a method that can work in your favor. Yet often interviewees intimidated by the power of the interviewer are overly conscious of the time they are taking, and tend to rush into their answers.

Many times a few seconds for thought will be a godsend. Asking for clarification is a good ploy to gain this thinking time. It gives you time to think about your answer while the interviewer is clearing up the ambiguity. You can also gain a little thinking time by using a bridge such as, "Let me see . . . " or "That's a good question . . . ."

If you have been asked a particularly difficult or weighty question, don't be afraid to take up extra time to consider your answer. The interviewer is talking to you because he is interested. He has budgeted time to talk with you, so the few extra seconds you spend formulating your thoughts will not be resented; they will probably be noted with approval.

The story of Dwight D. Eisenhower's interview with General George C. Marshall after the bombing of Pearl Harbor is a case in point. Marshall was looking for someone to command the forces in the Philippines and the Far East theater, and summoned Eisenhower to Washington for an interview.

When Germany invaded Poland in 1939 and World War II was finally unavoidable, Eisenhower was a lieutenant colonel and felt that even with the war and America's almost inevitable involvement, he had little prospects for advancement. Despite this feeling, two years later, on December 12, 1941, less than a week after the Japanese had bombed Pearl Harbor, Eisenhower had been promoted to brigadier general and was summoned to Washington by General Marshall, the chief of staff.

Eisenhower and Marshall had talked only twice before, once in 1930 and once in 1939. Marshall greeted Eisenhower perfunctorily and then outlined the stark situation that was facing the United States in the Pacific: the devastation of the Pacific fleet at Pearl, the invasion of the Philippines, the lack of any effective air strength, the damage caused by the Japanese army and air force, the critical supply shortage, the Japanese blockade. He painted a very grim picture of the situation. After he set the facts before Eisenhower, he looked Eisenhower in the eye and asked, "What should be our general line of action?"

Eisenhower was taken aback. He had just stepped off the plane and had no real personal knowledge of the situation. Here was the man who had to make the decision, a man who had been well-briefed and was on top of the situation, asking his opinion! Eisenhower was intuitive enough to recognize the importance of the question both for the war effort and for him personally. He said later, "His tone implied that I had been given the problem as a check to an answer he had already reached."

If ever an interviewee could have been pressured into giving an immediate answer, Eisenhower at that moment in history was the man. Here was the newly appointed chief of staff asking his opinion of the situation in the Philippines where Eisenhower had served for four years. Yet he kept his composure and did not reply off the top of his head. He asked General Marshall for a few hours to consider his answer.

Eisenhower returned later that afternoon with his recommendation: Even though the situation was almost hopeless from a military point of view, he felt that the United States should do everything possible in their defense. Marshall replied, "I agree with you. Do your best to save them."

Marshall's assessment of Eisenhower was undoubtedly based as much upon Eisenhower's method of answering the question as it was on the content of his answer. He wanted a man of judgment and depth, a man upon whom he could rely to make decisions based on analysis and cogitation. That Eisenhower displayed the confidence in himself to ask for time to formulate a reply must have impressed the chief.

This does not mean that you can ask for several hours before answering difficult questions in an interview. But it does illustrate the point that a few seconds of thoughtful silence before responding could be exactly what the interviewer is looking for.

Where to look

Where do you look during an interview? Should you always look the interviewer straight in the eye and stare him down? Should you look away? This is one of the real traumas many interviewees go through during an interview. Of course, the best advice is simply to act naturally. Talk with the interviewer as though you were having a cup of coffee with a friend.

Dr. Gerhard Nielson of Copenhagen conducted a study of how and where interviewees normally looked, and you should be aware of the results. He filmed interviews on a fast-running camera. In replaying the films in slow motion, his results showed that there is actually very little eye contact maintained during an interview. The most an interviewee looked at the interviewer was 73 percent of the time, which means that there was no eye contact 27 percent of the time. One man looked away for 92 percent of the time. Nielson found that half of the interviewees looked away for 50 percent of the time.

Nielson discovered other interesting things. When people are speaking, they tend to look away; when they are listening, they tend to maintain eye contact. It's normal for you not to look at the person to whom you are speaking. But I have found that interviewees worry about this and feel they should always look their interviewer in the eye. Yet, as Dr. Nielson's study found, this is abnormal. Being abnormal, it would strike the interviewer wrong and could very easily make him uncomfortable.

Nielson also discovered that interviewees tend to look away from the interviewer when they start to speak. There is a subtle timing in speaking, listening, looking, and looking away. Interviewees tend to look away just before or just after the beginning of one-quarter of their statements. Fifty percent of the interviewees look at the interviewer as they finish speaking.

Reader Jennifer Ruggaber of Syracuse, New York, quoted earlier, writes:

> As a shy person it makes me self-conscious and nervous to look the interviewer in the eyes. A trick I use that really works is to look at his nose. It is impossible to detect (except at very close range) and helps me to relax.

Don't worry about looking the interviewer in the eye. If you force it, it will come across unnaturally and leave a bad impression. Try to treat the interview as a conversation and act as you would in such a situation. The best rule is to act naturally and not worry about eye contact.

Eye signals

You should be aware of signals people make, often subconsciously, with their eyes. Even though neither party to a conversation may recognize the signals overtly, they may accept them as a nonverbal form of communication and act accordingly. You should be aware of these signals both as an interpretation for you to make of your interviewer and as signals you may be giving your interviewer.

Julius Fast, who has analyzed these signals in *Body Language*, explains that if you look away while you speak, it means that you're explaining yourself and shouldn't be interrupted. If you then look the other person in the eye, you are passing a signal to interrupt when you pause. But a pause without looking in the eye would mean that you aren't finished yet.

If you as a listener look away from a speaker, it indicates that you are dissatisfied with what is being said or that you are trying to conceal your reaction to the speaker's words. If you look away while you are speaking it may be interpreted to mean you are uncertain of what you're saying.

If you as a listener look at a speaker, it is a signal of agreement; and if you as a speaker look at a listener, it's a signal of confidence in what you say.

These are some assumptions that people may draw from your actions during conversation. Your actions may thus easily result in eliciting negative or positive reactions without your knowing exactly why.

Never forget that the important thing an interviewer derives from an interview is an intuitive feeling about you. It's either positive or negative. More often than not he will not be able to specify the exact reasons for his feeling, but he will have developed them nonetheless. It may be derived from how you have handled silence or how you've answered one question or how you've acted during the conversation. Whatever it is, it's your task to enhance a positive feeling. It is therefore important to be aware of the signals you make during conversation and the typical reaction of others to these signals.

You can also use this information to make judgments on your interviewer. You can make assumptions based on where, when, and how he looks when speaking and listening.

Eye signals are something of which you should be aware but I don't think they are especially important. What is important is that you act naturally and maintain a level of eye contact that is comfortable for you.

The premise that a person who is uncertain of what he or she is saying will look away while saying it is probably accurate. But to conclude that all people who look away while speaking are uncertain of what they are saying is absurd. Most people look away while speaking, and it's unrealistic to think that they are all doing so because of uncertainty.

They look away because that's the way most people naturally speak!

I mention Fast's ideas here simply because they add to your awareness of what's going on in an interview. If you're worried about whether you should concentrate on your eye signals or just forget them and act naturally, it's much better not to think about where you're looking and let your eyes fall where they may.

Treat every question as important

Interviews are generally short. Therefore, you must be sensitive enough to recognize that each question has significance and that you shouldn't answer offhandedly, thinking that the interviewer is just trying to make conversation.

Act as if every question the interviewer asks has a purpose. If the interviewer is inexperienced, he may well be just trying to make conversation and keep things moving. But you can't rely on this judgment. If you assume the interviewer knows what he is doing and that there is a purpose to all the questions, you won't be harmed. If you make the contrary assumption, you can be devastated. The purpose of the question may be hidden. A smart interviewer can determine many things from one response to one question.

Whenever you are tempted to throw away an answer, remember a story J. Paul Getty told about a test he once gave. He was concerned about cost consciousness at one of his companies, and decided to test the attitude of his three top executives. He instructed the payroll clerk to make a five dollar reduction in each of the executives' next paychecks, and told the clerk to send anyone who complained to Getty's office. Within an hour of distribution of the checks, all three executives were in Getty's office, complaining that their checks were short five dollars.

Getty pounced on them. He told them that there were so many inefficiencies in the company's operations that the company was losing tens of thousands of dollars. The executives were blind to these inefficiencies, but when the payroll department had an inefficiency that cost them five dollars, they were on it like a rabbit on a carrot. Getty reports that this test cost one of the executives his job. What seemed to be a simple thing to the executives was actually a career-testing confrontation.

Seemingly innocuous questions can have great bearing on the judgment an interviewer may make on you. One interviewee told me of a lesson he had learned by not being attuned to the fact that every remark or question an interviewer makes may be meaningful. He was being interviewed for a position as a trainee by the buyer to whom he would report for a major toy manufacturing company. As part of their selection process, he was required to take an IQ test. The interviewee had an IQ in excess of 150 and had the highest score ever achieved on the test.

The interviewer began by asking if the interviewee had been interviewing at many companies. The interviewee replied that he had been looking for a job for about a month. The interviewer offhandedly said, "I guess you're getting tired of these tests, eh?" to which the interviewee smiled and nodded.

The interview didn't last much longer and, thinking over why, the interviewee realized that he had been tricked into indicating that he really didn't have a high IQ, that he did well just because he had been taking the same test over and over. In fact it was the first IQ test he had taken since he had graduated from college. He had made a noncommittal response to the buyer's friendly intimation merely to be agreeable. His failure to be alert to provide accurate information to the question had cost him.

His response should have been along the following lines. "No, this is the first such test I have taken since I was a sophomore in college and I was somewhat surprised to find that you would require an IQ test for this position. Do you find that it adequately tests for an aptitude for being a buyer?"

This response not only gets across the fact that the test score was an accurate measure of IQ, but it puts the interviewer in the difficult position of defending the use of the test to a person who had scored very highly on it. If the interviewer does defend the accuracy of the test, how can he logically reject an applicant who had scored so well, at least on that basis?

This answer, however, carries a greater risk than most, because the challenge is pretty aggressive. Basically, the interviewee is challenging not only the interviewer, but the company's entire selection format. An answer like this could cause the interviewer to think, "Who is this person, a job applicant, challenging the criteria we have set for this position?" And this kind of thinking could lead on to a negative response to the essential question each interviewer has, "Do I want someone like this working for me?" If your goal is to create the impression that you would be an agreeable person in the organization, this type of response could be extremely damaging. This dilemma is just an example of the many decisions with which you are faced when you are in a person-to-person interview situation and the solution lies in the personal assessment you have made of the interviewer by this stage of the interview. Since, in this instance, it was the first question asked, the interviewee was shooting from the hip, and that's probably why he answered the way he did, and his timidity cost him the interview. At the first stage of the interview, a better response would be a simple straightforward denial, "No, this is the first IQ test I've taken since I was a sophomore in college," with no challenge.

Unfair questions

Life, as John F. Kennedy once said, is not fair. Sometimes you'll be presented with a situation by a prospective employer that is eminently unfair. Colman Andrews, a restaurant writer for the *Los Angeles Times*, reported the following story about the manager of a tony private club in Los Angeles:

> One day, one of his better busboys came to him during the breakfast service and asked when he might be allowed to graduate to waiter status. "I'll get you a jacket and you can go on the floor right now," he replied, "if you can answer one question for me: What varieties of fruit are in the assorted fruit tray today?"

The bus boy was unprepared for the question and couldn't answer it. "When you start paying attention to details like that without anybody asking you to," he told the aspiring waiter, "come ask me about being a waiter again."

What the busboy replied is not on record.

When I first read this story I was outraged and I'm still outraged now, years later, as I write this. Here was a person starting out as the lowest employee in the restaurant chain, a busboy, cleaning off tables. But he had ambition and showed it by approaching his boss and asking a simple question; he didn't need an impudent reply.

There were two conclusions the busboy could draw from the reply. One was that the reply was absolutely designed to put him in his place and keep him there instead of encouraging his ambition. As a busboy there was no requirement or need for him to know what kind of fruit was in the assorted fruit tray since his job was limited to cleaning off tables after the food had been eaten. So to ask a busboy something totally unrelated to his job was completely unfair. Besides, a wise manager wouldn't want his busboys wasting their time looking at the fruit trays every day to see what was on them. What for? That's not going to make them better busboys. Further, it's difficult to imagine that the manager of an exclusive private club would promote a busboy to a waiter just because the busboy knew what was in the fruit tray that day. There's certainly more to being a waiter than that. So it's most likely that the manager was just being a wise guy and making a cruel joke at his busboy's expense, that he could later relate to a nationally prominent writer who could then poke fun at the poor busboy.

The other conclusion the busboy could draw was that the manager was a wise person and he was answering his question specifically. And that's the initial conclusion the busboy should have drawn from the answer because, if you draw two conclusions from an answer, one of which requires no action to test the conclusion and the other allows action that could test the conclusion, you should adopt the latter. Even though the likelihood of this conclusion being accurate was slight, the busboy had little to lose by adopting and testing it and little to gain by taking offense at being made the butt of a joke.

So, taking the manager's answer literally, the busboy could make it a point to check each day on the fruit tray, then, a couple of weeks later, approach the manager with the same question about becoming a waiter. If the manager is an honest person, he would then take steps toward promoting the busboy. If he puts the busboy off once again, the busboy will know that the manager is a dishonest person and that he has no future working for him. He could start looking for another job with someone he could count on to reward his ambition and competence. Short of getting a job, what could be a better result of an interview than to discover the low character of the person for whom you would be working?

But not all restaurant managers are as arrogant and insensitive as the preceding one. Patrick Terrail, who established Ma Maison restaurant in Los Angeles, which was so successful it had an unlisted telephone number and was frequented by the Who's Who of Hollywood, developed a list of test questions applicants had to answer when applying for a job as a waiter:

1. Describe the service procedure in four or five steps for serving a bottle of red wine;

2. List four jobs a waiter should do before the restaurant opens;

3. List in order of importance to you the reasons for a successful restaurant;

4. True or False:

   a. A guest is not the person who makes it possible for us to earn our salary;

   b. A guest is dependent on us, we are not depending on them;

   c. Waiters should chew gum while working at the restaurant.

It's no wonder that Patrick Terrail is successful. But when you're an interviewee, you must be prepared for both the good and the bad. If you discover the bad, you've done a good interview. I just hope that you have the courage and financial capability to reject the bad when you discover it. Sometimes you must take whatever is offered, but at least, if you've done a good interview, you will know the character of the person for whom you are working and will be able to act accordingly.

The throwaway joke

The many interviews I have conducted over the years tend to run together in my mind, but naturally a few stand out for one reason or another. One fellow I interviewed for a position with a client gave me a classic answer when I asked him what he felt his biggest asset was. "I had my wife interview me last night," he said. "That was one of the questions she asked and we discussed how to answer it. I guess my biggest asset is that I'm always on time."

I was nonplussed. Here was an entrée for him to tell of his most glowing achievement. He could have picked anything from when he won his high school debating medal to his courage on the battlefield to his industriousness, morality, candor, likability. Anything. Instead he used this opportunity to crack a joke.

Revealing that he had gone through a mock interview was a calculated risk. Naturally it's better to try to appear spontaneous, but to admit that you've prepared as much as this is not necessarily a negative. It shows the interviewer that you care enough to do some homework, and that's all to the good. Another point in his favor was that he was perceptive enough to anticipate a question that generally takes interviewees by surprise. Up to this point, he was doing well.

But then he blew the opportunity. His answer indicated two things to me. First, the easy judgment is to accept the answer at face value. His biggest asset is that he's on time. If that's the case, I don't want him. I want someone who has more to offer than that. The second possibility is that he's making a joke. In that case, I want him even less. Here is a man undergoing an interview that could change his life. He is asked a serious question, one that is obviously meaningful to his interviewer and begs for an intelligent response. Yet his response is a flip joke. This indicates a shallow, insensitive individual with whom I would never entrust serious problems.

I did not offer this man a job. I did interview him again to ensure that my initial judgment was correct. In this second interview he launched into a monologue that lasted an hour and fifteen minutes. My first impression was confirmed: the man had an abrasive personality and was insensitive. Even so, I checked the two references he gave me. Both were surprised that they had been given as references and, under probing questioning, revealed their dissatisfaction with his personality and his ability to get along with others.

Here was a man who had three opportunities and flunked all three. Had he answered the question he had anticipated more maturely, perhaps I never would have received the vibrations that I did. But then, that's the purpose of an interview and it is what separates the good interviewer from the bad and the good interviewee from the bad.

Humor is not necessarily bad in an interview. The first time George Martin got the Beatles together for a recording session, Martin, trying to make them feel comfortable, explained what was going to occur and told them if they didn't like anything to let him know. George Harrison replied, "Well, for a start, I don't like your tie." This joke worked (even though it was Martin's favorite tie) and contributed to his positive feeling about their charm. Harrison's joke did not occur at the beginning of the interview, though, but after they had spent a considerable amount of time with each other. In addition, the Beatles were entertainers and spontaneous humor is part of the job. Further, Martin's question was not a serious, probing one, but was clearly meant to put them at ease. Harrison's joke told him that he had done so without saying it in so many words.

So humor can be used if it is at an appropriate time and in good taste. Avoid poking fun at your interviewer, as it can be insulting and the probability is that it will not inspire empathy. If you feel the need, it is better to make yourself the butt of the joke because you will not hurt yourself by offending your interviewer. Whether or not you use humor depends on whether or not you can recognize the right spot and are mature enough not to use a serious question as a straight line for a comedy routine.

The blockbuster question

Sometimes an interview will start with a real blockbuster of a question. The one that I think is the most difficult by far is "Tell me about yourself." You think that looks easy and innocuous? Have it sprung on you at the beginning of an interview for a job you desperately want and then see if you think it's so simple.

What do you say? Do you repeat what's on the résumé? Do you tell about your love life? Talk about your outside interests?

If you've done your preparation, you know something about the interviewer, the company, and the job. You know what you want to say in the interview. Try to formulate an answer to this question **before** you go into the interview so that you can jump right into it. It is actually a terrific opportunity to take charge of the interview and talk about your strengths.

You can talk about accomplishments of which you're most proud. You can talk of your qualifications and why you think you want the job and why you think you would do a good job. You can say anything you want.

A question of this sort also tells you that the interviewer may be fairly sophisticated. By putting you in control of the interview at the outset, he can be making judgments on you right away, not only from the content of your answer but from **how** you choose to answer.

On this subject, reader Dr. Daniel J. Fink, vice president and medical director of AmeriMed of Burbank, California, writes:

> A friend of mine was applying for a psychiatry residency, so I offered to do a practice interview with him. By the time we could set up the hour, he had already interviewed at the prestigious university teaching hospital he really wanted to attend. I began our interview by asking him how his interview had gone. "Not too well," he replied. The three interviews with faculty members had gone well—not overwhelmingly positive, but not overwhelmingly negative. The last interview, though, had been a disaster. The chief resident asked him, "Tell me about yourself," and he responded, "I'm just a plain schmuck like anyone else." The interview had gone downhill from there. I gently explained to my friend that in Yiddish "schmuck" was slang for penis—most closely translated into English as "prick." **The lessons: don't use words you don't understand, and be prepared to answer open-ended questions.**
>
> Another friend was being interviewed for admission to medical school by the admissions dean, a man nationally known for in-

timidating applicants. The interview had gone very well until the dean asked my friend, "What field do you think you might be interested in?" My friend, who actually was and still is quite socially conscious but was trying to appear even more so, answered, "Community medicine." "That's great," the dean responded. "Tell me what you mean by community medicine." My friend, who really did not know, was speechless. **Lesson: Don't say something unless you mean it. If you are going to say it, especially when it's not entirely true, be able to answer questions about it.**

Dual-purpose questions

Questions are often asked for reasons other than are apparent from their content. For instance, the question, "What have you done of which you are most proud?" seems to ask you to tell of some outstanding accomplishment. But there is more to it. The question probes, on an unstated level, your ability to make a decision. A question such as this is calculated to flood the mind with recall of many accomplishments. An indecisive person may be unable to decide which achievement to discuss. In a situation like this, you should choose one and talk of it, even though there may be many things you've done in the past of which you are proud. This will show that you are a decisive person, able to make up your mind quickly.

Questions about your private life

Sometimes interviewers will ask insensitive questions about your private life, probing not only areas about marriage, but also lovers and so on. This commonly happens in interviews for real estate sales positions in which the rationale of the interviewer is that he wants to be sure that, if offered a position, you will devote sufficient time to selling real estate.

We cover unlawful pre-employment inquiries in Chapters 11 and 13. While you should be familiar with what the law allows, you should also use your common sense in determining whether a personal question is appropriate or relevant.

I don't think it's ever appropriate to answer questions of this sort. Questions like, "Do you have a boyfriend [girlfriend]? Do you spend weekends together?" are nobody's business but yours. They have no relation to your job, and nobody has a right to butt into your personal affairs. Interviewees are generally so docile that they will answer such questions. For one thing, going through an interview is not unlike going through a lie-detector test. Furthermore, most interviewees are afraid they will blow their chances for a job offer if they do not reply.

Balderdash! When you are asked a question that is off-limits, you should have the courage to say honestly, but without rancor, that you're applying for this position because you feel it's something you want to do. If you were not planning on devoting sufficient time to performing the duties required, you wouldn't be taking the interviewer's time, and your own, to apply and go through the interview process. What you do in your private life and with your free time will have no effect on how you perform the functions of the position.

A reply like this serves notice that you know the interviewer is skating on thin ice, so he may accept a gentle rebuff. But you can't be so sensitive that you have a whole list of questions you won't answer. If it's a major point and if your objection is legitimate, it's perfectly acceptable to decline to answer. But if you do it too often, you have either had the misfortune of being interviewed by Attila the Hun, or you're too sensitive and will encounter great difficulties in getting beyond the first interview.

In any event, don't let the interviewer intimidate you and push you around. Your private life is private and is of no legitimate concern to him.

Skeletons in your closet

Virtually everyone has at least one skeleton in the closet that could be a source of embarrassment. If yours is job or school related, there is a fairly good chance that the interviewer will strike upon it. You should prepare your response very carefully on this point because an unexpected thrust at a vulnerable area can be devastating.

For instance, assume that you left one of your previous jobs because you had a fight with your supervisor. Assume further that you had worked there for a considerable period of time, so you can't omit the job from your résumé. It's possible that an interviewer will ask you why you left. You must be able to respond to this question honestly but in a way that places you in a favorable light.

You should review the circumstances of the situation and come up with a truthful explanation that cannot be contradicted by a reference check. On your side is the fact that previous employers are reluctant to give out derogatory information on former employees, so the facts of the situation may be difficult for your interviewer to discover from any other source. It is helpful, however, for you to know what kind of a reference you will be given. You may have a friend make a check on you with the prior employer to discover how a real reference check will be handled. Knowing this, you can face an interviewer with a fair degree of confidence how an inquiry by him will be received and tailor your response accordingly.

It is not a bad answer to say that you had a personality conflict with your supervisor and were unable to work it out so you felt that it was better for both you and the company if you left. That's all right to explain one departure on your record. But if you use it more than once, the interviewer may decide that you are a difficult person to get along with—and this can be the kiss of death. Just about everyone has had one or two people with whom they have had personality conflicts and have been unable to get along. But if you've had this unfortunate circumstance more than once, you will be at a disadvantage if the subject comes up in an interview. As a result, you had better have another honest, verifiable reason for leaving more than one job. This is where preparation is most important. Your answer must be honest. If this is your skeleton, you must be prepared for it. It may not arise, but if it does and you haven't planned for it well in advance, the likelihood of your surviving the question is slim.

Of course, you may have other skeletons. If there's something that you hope you won't be asked, you should know exactly what you're going to say if he **does** ask you about that. This is another area where your demeanor in answering the question will be almost as important as the words you use. If it appears to the interviewer that you're equivocating or lack confidence in your response, it won't matter much what you say. The impression you leave will probably be negative. So know how you're going to respond and respond with confidence and candor.

Admitting a weakness can be disarming. An answer along the following lines assumes responsibility and gets the point across without saying anything negative: "You know, he just had the type of personality that was very difficult for me to get along with. I like to be able to admire and respect the people I work for, but there was something about him that I felt was wrong. I handled the situation very poorly because my attitude seemed to be communicated to him and it alienated him, so he treated me in a manner that I felt to be unacceptable. I blame myself for this entirely and have felt badly about it. Since I recognized that he rubbed me the wrong way, I probably should have been able to work out our differences in some manner that would have been agreeable to both of us. But it was a very difficult situation for me. I was so close to the situation, so emotionally involved, that I was unable to take an objective view of it and it just seemed to get worse. Looking back, I can see some things that I probably should have done to alleviate the situation, but the best that I can say now is that I learned from the experience and if it ever arose again, I think I'd be better capable of handling it."

Answering a question in that way will show that you accept full responsibility for the situation. Even if you don't feel responsible for the problem, this type of answer will place you in the best light and will protect you against a bad reference check. Basically you're saying, "This guy was a jerk, but I should have been able to handle that. Therefore it's my fault and I'll know how to deal with it if there's a next time." On the other hand, if you tell the interviewer, "The guy was an absolute loser—no one could get along with him—I had finally had him up to here and told him to shove it," and on a reference check, the interviewer gets a similar response about you, the interviewer, not knowing who to believe, will probably conclude that it's not worth the risk of hiring a potentially disagreeable person and reject you.

Don't keep fighting the battle. If you accept the responsibility and say that you learned from the experience, you disarm any negative things that may be said about you and project an image of peacemaker rather than warrior.

Grievances against former employers

Don't criticize a former employer. The advice your mother gave you, "If you can't say anything nice about someone, don't say anything," applies here. Even if you have a legitimate grievance against someone, don't talk about it. If you are asked, just say something that will dissuade further questions. You can turn the interviewer away from the subject with a tactful answer like, "I don't feel it's fair to them for me to discuss our disagreements with other people." This will not only turn away any further inquiries; the interviewer should consider you a person of discretion.

I had an interview with a potential client once who had a great deal of lucrative legal work that she needed to have done. We discussed the details of the work and then I asked her about her prior attorney. This loosed a wave of virulence about the lawyer. She castigated him for every indiscretion of which she could think: he overcharged; he did poor and sloppy work; he was never available to talk with her; he continually pressed her to pay his exorbitant fees. Her diatribe went on for fifteen minutes.

The impression she made upon me was completely different from that which she had intended. My conclusion was that no matter how much work she had for me, she would feel that she owned me. She would call anytime, day or night. If I happened to be working on other problems, she wouldn't understand. Finally, she would eventually be sitting in some other lawyer's office talking of me as she was now talking of her last lawyer. I declined the client mainly on the strength of the feeling I developed during her criticism of her former attorney.

An interviewer can be expected to form the same sort of judgment if you severely criticize a former employer. He will probably conclude that hiring you isn't worth the risk and reject you. He doesn't want to hire someone who will be sitting in another interviewer's office a year hence complaining about him.

If you refuse to discuss your grievances, you improve your position. Even if a check of the situation results in a negative report, it's probable that the interviewer will respect you for not talking against someone with whom you have had problems, and the empathy thus gained may be enough to overcome any negative feelings your antagonist may have been able to arouse in the interviewer.

Of course, if the interviewer presses you, you have no choice but to give your side of the story. A refusal on your part could leave the impression that you have something to hide. This, buttressed by a negative report from your antagonist, would probably be enough to cause a rejection.

If the interviewer refuses to allow you to drop the subject, explain the situation in as dispassionate a manner as possible. Some interviewers will probe such points not to discover the facts of the situation or to find out who was right or wrong. They may be examining your ability to maintain control in an emotional situation. If you become emotional while telling the story, it could indicate that you lack self-control, and this could result in a negative inference. Although you want to present your case in a forceful enough manner to counterbalance your antagonist's story, you want to do it as unemotionally as you can.

CHECKLIST

★ The most important aspect that an interviewer gets out of an interview is a subjective feeling about the interviewee.
★ You must enhance that feeling.
★ Listen to the question.

* If the question is ambiguous, you should either interpret it in your way and say what puts you in the best light or ask for a clarification.

* Use ploys to get thinking time: ask for a clarification or use a bridge.

* Don't worry about thinking for a few seconds before you answer.

* Don't worry about eye contact; just act naturally.

* Assume that every question is asked for a purpose.

* Be ready for the blockbuster question.

* Handle the offensive question firmly but tactfully.

* Tactfully decline to answer questions about your private life.

* Prepare good answers for questions that may probe skeletons in your closet.

* Find out how your references will respond to a check.

* Accept responsibility for personality conflicts.

* Don't put the interviewer in the middle of a battle.

* Don't talk against a former employer.

* If you must discuss a bad situation with a former employer, do so dispassionately.

* Answer specific questions specifically.

* Don't respond to a serious question with a flip joke.

* If you joke, don't make the interviewer the butt of it.

* Recognize dual purpose questions and answer them decisively.

ASSUMPTIONS

Reactions can be illogical. It is almost impossible to determine in advance how an interviewer is going to respond (and for this chapter, let's assume the interviewer is a woman). An interviewee takes a particular risk when she assumes an aggressive position with someone whom she has known for less than ten minutes.

When an interviewee shows up for an interview with me, dressed in a slovenly manner, I generally ask about it. One time the response I received was, "I want people to judge me for the kind of person I am, not for the clothes I wear. Do you think it mattered what Clarence Darrow wore?" The interviewee sat back smugly, thinking that he had scored a tremendous point. He had assumed that my immediate reaction would be to conjure up an image of Darrow defending a great cause in his studiedly unkempt dress. Unfortunately, he was wrong.

Instead, it brought to mind images of Earl Rogers, a renowned trial lawyer of early twentieth-century Los Angeles, called by many the father of demonstrative evidence and the witness box dénouement so often seen in Perry Mason mysteries.

When Darrow was indicted for bribery in the Los Angeles Times bombing case, Rogers got him acquitted in a brilliant defense. Rogers's trademark was to show up in court dressed in formal evening wear, and that's what I thought of when my smug interviewee mentioned Darrow. Irrelevant? Illogical? Perhaps. But an interviewee has no way of knowing how an interviewer will react to an assertion. This particular interviewee obviously assumed I shared his belief that Clarence Darrow was the Mahatma of the legal profession. Because his assumption was wrong, his thrust was not just impotent, it created a negative feeling in me.

This epitomizes the great risk we all take in the interview process. The person conducting the interview is a stranger. We cannot hope to discover much about her—her education, intelligence, and prejudices. We are at sea in a world of uncertainty. For this reason, if for no other, we must base our actions on facts as we perceive them in the short period of time at our disposal. To venture into the unknown by making rhetorical parries is to step into an abyss. You may hit the bull's-eye and score grandly. On the other hand, the odds are much in favor of missing the mark and creating a negative feeling that no amount of rehabilitation can overcome.

Observe the interviewer

What is positive for one interviewer may be negative for another. For instance, Dr. Robert Langrod, when he was president of Bertea Corporation, said, "I'm not looking for quick, fast responses. I'm looking for responses that are logical and make sense." On the other hand, Paul Moller, who was president of USA Petroleum Corporation, had an entirely different view. "I interviewed a man I hired about two months ago. He really came across like a go-getter. Any question I asked he had a quick reply. He never had to hesitate. Some people have to hesitate on a question. He never hesitated. He knew the answer right away. That really impressed me."

So, unless you have advance knowledge of your interviewer's prejudices on any point, you will have to size her up quickly during the interview. You should pay very close attention to her and be sensitive to her reactions to you.

The perceptive person can detect hints others give that subconsciously communicate their feelings. Sharyn Cole of the Los Angles Bonaventure Hotel says, "I don't consciously use body language myself. But if an interviewee knew what he was doing, I'm sure that it would work. If I sit up straight, it means that the interviewee is getting on my nerves, or I'm getting defensive. If I sit back it means I'm relaxed and that would be a good sign for the interviewee."

Each interviewer may be different, but they will all give clues as to how you are being received. You should be perceptive enough to observe these clues and adjust your interview accordingly.

If you notice what seems to be a negative response— the interviewer is sitting up straight, fidgeting, folding her arms, or looking away while you are talking—you should take the hint and either stop talking or change the subject. If you strongly feel that the body language of the interviewer is telling you that you are not being well received in what you are doing, don't compound the problem by continuing. When some people perceive they are not being well received, they become nervous and talk too much. If you have the perception to read the body language, use it to your advantage and stop doing whatever it might be that is causing negative reactions.

Superficial assumptions

You must be sensitive, however, that you do not make an assumption based upon a superficial observation of your interviewer. Many times the true situation is far different than it appears to be at first glance.

A few years ago when I was engaged in a negotiation with another lawyer, I instantly developed a negative attitude toward him because he wouldn't look me in the eye; he always seemed to be gazing at a spot just over my left shoulder. This grated on my nerves, and I took it for a sign of weakness and uncertainty on his part.

A few months later I was spending the weekend with a friend and her family in Old Greenwich, Connecticut. She had her college roommate over for dinner, and her roommate looked at me exactly as had the lawyer I considered weak and uncertain. My reaction was similarly negative. As the evening progressed my friend brought up the fact that her roommate was wall-eyed, and it had caused her no end of self-consciousness.

I felt mortified and guilty. Clearly my judgment on the lawyer was wrong. He had the same problem, and I had made an assumption without establishing the facts. By this injustice I had insensitively rejected him for a reason that didn't exist. In fact, it took a great strength of character for him to persevere in a profession where eye contact is so important and, for him, virtually impossible.

It's difficult to judge things solely by using a factual basis without making assumptions. But it's essential that your reactions and actions in an interview be based upon facts to the largest extent possible. In addition to their inherent inequity, erroneous assumptions acted upon can be disastrous.

One reader, who asks to remain anonymous, writes:

I'd never heard of a "stress interview" until I read your book. Two years ago a major corporation spent $200 to bring me up from Los Angeles to San Francisco for an interview. It was a panel interview. The three people who interviewed me were so hostile from the minute I walked into the room that I assumed that seeing a middle-aged woman arrive, they were angry at having spent $200 to bring me there. Their questions were, from the outset, designed to put me on the defensive, i.e., "What makes you think you can do such-and-such?", etc. One of the interviewers even asked me why I'd dared to send them a letter typed with dirty typewriter keys!

I was certain, afterwards, that my age was a factor in my not being offered the job. I'd never heard of a "stress interview" until reading *Sweaty Palms*. But *Sweaty Palms* has quite literally changed my life. It made me realize how I've messed up in past interviews because I'd *assumed* when I didn't get the job I interviewed for that it was because of my age (55). Realizing that in all probability it was *another* reason (my not handling some aspect of the interview as well as I should have) has lifted a burden from my shoulders. What a relief it is to forget about age in an interview and concentrate instead on what the interviewer's saying and how she's saying it—and on my own responses.

When "yes" doesn't mean "I agree"

Don't delude yourself that the interviewer agrees with everything you're saying merely because she nods agreement. You can easily be led down the primrose path by your assumption that you've hit upon a common belief when in reality her reaction may not signify agreement at all. Averell Harriman had an especially close relationship with President Franklin Roosevelt during World War II, and he commented on Roosevelt's penchant for using the word "yes" when he didn't really mean "I agree."

> Lack of understanding of what the President means when he nods or says "yes" has led to much bitterness on the part of . . . businessmen who assume they have the agreement of the President when all they have, really, is an indication that the President is not prepared to argue the point with them. . . . It means that he hears and understands what you are saying, but not necessarily that he agrees to it. Anyone who assumes otherwise is engaging in wishful thinking, or is not very astute.

A nod of the head or a brief "yes" may mean just the opposite of agreement: it may be a signal that the interviewer has heard all she wishes to hear of that subject and wishes you to get on to something else.

Analysis of specific technique

One of the most sophisticated interviewing techniques was that used some years ago by the Life Sciences Division of

Whittaker Corporation in performing their contract with the Saudi Arabian government to provide hospital and related services in Saudi Arabia. They needed to hire specialized individuals, such as doctors, nurses, technicians, and administrators who were of a high caliber.

The positions in Saudi Arabia had many negative factors, the primary one being a tremendous culture shock. Thus the selection process became a most important componet of Whittaker's performance. Each hire cost the division approximately $10,000. Therefore, if someone was hired who did not fulfill the minimum contract time period of eighteen months in Saudi Arabia, the mistake was extremely costly to the company. Not only were they out the $10,000 it cost them to make a selection, they lost a significant period of time and performance.

Jerry Kenefick was the manager of the international recruitment office of the division. His staff consisted entirely of professionals in the fields for which they were interviewing. Doctors interviewed doctors, nurses interviewed nurses, and so on.

They received approximately sixty résumés a day from all over the United States. Ninety percent were from people who were obviously not qualified. The remaining 10 percent were prescreened by telephone; this interview eliminated 95 percent of the remaining 10 percent. So out of the résumés received, 0.05 percent were invited in for the second-stage interview.

Cheryl Vanos, the logistics coordinator, characterized the interview as a "negative-stress" one—that is, the negative aspects of the position were stressed to weed out those who would not survive the tour of duty.

Kenefick said that although their interview process was designed to pick those who were not only qualified but who would be able to adjust to the Saudi lifestyle, the final decision was based upon a feeling that he and the other interviewers had about the candidate. He can't define how he arrived at his feeling but stated that it was generally accurate and that he and the other interviewers usually arrived at this feeling within the first ten minutes of the interview.

Kenefick's interview consisted of two parts. Initially he looked for qualifications, so he would go down the résumé with the interviewee item by item. If he discovered a gap or an inconsistency, he'd ask about it. Any intentional misrepresentation could seriously damage a candidate's chances.

The second phase was to determine if the interviewee was the right kind of person to go to Saudi Arabia. He asked many questions to get to the inner person; What do you do in your spare time? Do you have close friends? When was the last time you got together? What was the last movie you saw? He probed these areas because Saudi Arabian society is spartan by American standards. There are no movies, no churches, no television.

Interviewees generally tried to give answers they felt the interviewer was looking for. A typical answer was, "I read, never watch TV, don't go to movies, and like to be by myself." Kenefick would let this pass and then later in the interview (which lasted from forty-five minutes to four hours, depending on the level of the position) would gently ask if the interviewee happened to see a certain television show or movie. Normally it turned out that the interviewee did like television or movies or American sports and answered the way she did only to get the job.

Kenefick used other ploys to get candidates to eliminate themselves. "Once," he said, "I had an interviewee who was dressed very fastidiously. Everything was perfect from his hair style to his shoelaces. As we talked, I dwelt on the size of the roaches over there, the fact that the flour moved constantly because of the weevils, things like that. The interviewee actually had to excuse himself as I was talking because it upset him so. He came back and said that he didn't think he was interested."

If the candidate got by Kenefick, she went to the final stage by meeting with Vanos, whose ostensible job was to brief the candidate on life in Saudi Arabia.

"The interviewee has been through an entire day of interviewing with Jerry and the others," she said. "He gets to me and thinks that it's all over. So he tends to relax and drop his pretensions. He doesn't realize that I'm assessing him, too. He may confide his trepidations to me. Or he may inadvertently let me see what he's really like. After I'm through with him, I'll get together with Jerry if I have some doubts about him, and several times a candidate has been rejected because of my input. We have to be very sure that the person we hire will stick it out and perform in an acceptable manner once he gets over there.

"I remember one fellow who we were interviewing as hospital administrator. He got to talking about his daughter and her fiancé. He exhibited a very low tolerance for her fiancé's goals and ideas. He came across as very inflexible. Well, how's he going to react when his forty-year-old head nurse comes to him and complains that she's been caught by the Saudi religious police for living with some American engineer and is going to be deported? She will be crying that she's forty years old, recently divorced and lonely, that she needs companionship. How's he going to deal with that if he doesn't have the tolerance to cope with his daughter's fiancé and his contrary ideas and lifestyle?"

Kenefick said that he probed candidates' motivations for wanting to go to Saudi Arabia. "Invariably," he said, "they say that they want to go for three reasons. One, they want to do good for Saudi Arabia. Two, they want to travel. Three, they have an adventurous spirit.

"My job is to get beyond these three reasons to the real reason. Are they running away from a divorce or an unhappy love affair? Why do they *really* want to go? Not that their reasons that they give initially aren't what they believe. They are generally highly motivated people and these are real reasons. But we know that there quite often is some other reason and if there is, we want to know what that is. Saudi Arabia is no place to recover from a broken heart."

Vanos wanted to hear "that they were motivated by money. Because in Saudi Arabia, when you have to be there for from eighteen months to two years, money is the thing that keeps you going in the final analysis. If they admit this, we can be more confident that their motivations are such that they will last for the term of their contract."

There are several lessons to be learned from this. First, always make the assumption that you are going to be exposed to a good, sophisticated interview technique on the part of the interviewer. Even though the chances are that the interviewer won't be as competent as Kenefick and his crew, if you prepare for the best, you'll be ready for anything.

Second, assume that every question is asked for a reason connected with the job, even if it sounds like idle chatter. The man who sharply criticized his daughter's fiancé didn't realize that this was being projected by the interviewer to an actual job situation and a judgment made thereon.

Third, don't assume that just because you're talking to someone other than the person who makes the final hiring decision, the interview is over. The interview lasts until you have accepted an offer or been finally rejected. Remember, there's many a slip 'twixt the tongue and the lip. Even though they make up their minds on you once, they can change at any stage.

Table manners

You are **always** being evaluated whenever you are in the presence of the interviewer or anyone connected with the interviewer. Often an interview will include a meal. Don't be misled into believing that this is a "break," a time to relax, to let your hair down. Not only is this still a part of the interview, it might be the **most important** part. As a result, it's important to develop good table manners. I recommend buying a book on etiquette, like *Miss Manners' Guide to Excruciatingly Correct Behavior* or *Amy Vanderbilt's Everyday Etiquette*. But some common rules are:

1. Be on time. Miss Manners says that there is "no excuse for being late to a business luncheon short of having been run over on the way there."

2. Introduce **everyone** in the group. If you don't, you will inevitably insult someone.

3. Don't fake pronunciation of menu items. If the menu is in a foreign language and you are unfamiliar with it and there's no English translation, ask for an explanation. Feigning knowledge makes you look ridiculous and could result in a negative inference that could cost you a job offer. If you can't pronounce or don't know what something is, just ask. Nobody will ever forget you if you order steak tartare well done, but you'll wish they would. Showing that you are not afraid to reveal that you don't know something is an indication that you are comfortable with

yourself as you are and are not pretending to be something you are not.

4. Don't put your arms on the table.

5. Don't talk with food in your mouth.

6. Take the time to learn how to use the proper utensils. The general rule is that you work from the outside in. If there is more than one fork, for example, you use the outside fork for the first course, usually a small fork for the salad. Then after the salad and salad fork are removed, you use the next fork, the larger one, for the main course. It's easy if you know the rules.

7. Never force someone to have another drink, dessert, or whatever. Let the others make up their own minds.

8. Don't put your briefcase or carrying case on the table. *Gauche* floods to the mind. Not a bad idea, however, to have your pen and notebook handy, as mentioned previously. Just don't set them on the table.

9. Don't pick up the check unless it's your obligation. The general rule is that whoever invites, pays. And this is true regardless of sex.

10. Don't complain publicly in front of your companions about the service. If there's a problem and it's your responsibility, excuse yourself from the table and, instead of confronting the miscreant privately, lodge your complaint with the maître d'.

Good manners consist of simple common courtesy. If you're thoughtful and considerate of your companions and think of their comfort before your own, you will be on the road to being well mannered.

Reader Dr. Daniel Fink, quoted earlier, tells of a case directly in point:

> We just had a bizarre experience interviewing a potential vice president. First, we are a "shirt-sleeves" organization, at least in the office, and the candidate declined to remove his suit coat, despite the fact that the president and I were both in our shirt-sleeves. Second, the interview had been set for 11:00 a.m. so we could have an informal working lunch. The candidate declined to join us, stating that he had eaten a big breakfast, and sat drinking a glass of water while we ate our sandwiches. Even though he is qualified in terms of experience, we wonder how he would fit in. If the host-interviewer offers food or drink, I think the interviewee should at least accept something, perhaps just a salad or a bowl of soup and a diet drink, even if he doesn't finish it.

Physical impairments

Reader Thomas A. Ruhoff of Tucson, Arizona writes:

> I was scheduled for interviews on Thursday and Friday. On Wednesday I came down with a recurrence of Bell's palsy, in which one side of the face is temporarily paralyzed. The paralysis was most noticeable to myself, but other people said they did not notice it at all—until I smiled. I was advised to not tell the interviewer about my condition. I did not think it wise to let him or her draw undue conclusions, for instance that I had had a stroke and would need long-term medical care. In both interviews I started off by explaining why my face did not work and emphasized that it was a transient condition. Both interviewers thanked me for telling them about the palsy and then we went on with the rest on the interview.

Mr. Ruhoff's way of handling his impairment was perfect. Because interviewers generally form impressions based more on the way they feel about an interviewee rather than the empirical data derived during the interview, it would be unwise to let the affliction pass with no comment. It's clearly not in your best interests for the interviewer to draw a negative inference that might be much worse than the actual cause. Further, even if the interviewer didn't conclude that you had a permanent affliction, the conclusion might be more vague, and that could be even worse. For the interviewer to come away thinking, "I didn't like that person" without knowing why can be worse than coming away thinking, "maybe he's got a permanent affliction." The latter can be overcome. To combat the former is Herculean.

Don't key your performance to assumptions

The Whittaker interview process described earlier clearly illustrates two disadvantages of making assumptions not based on fact and trying to key your performance to those assumptions. If your assumptions are correct and you play the role so well that you get the job, when you return to your normal self, you won't be happy with the job and the employer won't be happy with you. You'll be worse off than if you had never gotten the job. And if your assumptions are wrong, and they were actually looking for someone just like you, you could role-play yourself out of an opportunity.

Never answer a question just to please the interviewer. You must come across as yourself, an honest person who knows himself or herself, and is comfortable that way.

This doesn't mean you should ever be rude. Your honesty does not diminish if you back off from a subject or manner of acting when you observe that it is not being well received. Would you tell Julie Andrews how much you detested *The Sound of Music*? Discretion does not imply dishonesty. Rather, it is simple courtesy.

False conclusions

Never walk out of an interview and say, "Boy, did I do lousy there! I'm sure I made a bad impression and blew my chance." How do you know how the interviewer reacted to you? You really don't know what she was looking for. You may have connected on all cylinders, yet you're projecting your standards upon her and making the assumption that you failed.

Dr. Robert H. Schuller, in his book *Move Ahead with Possibility Thinking*, relates a classic story about a Chinese man who had one horse and one son that points out the errors of assuming. The horse ran away and the neighbors commiserated on his bad luck.

"Why," the old Chinese said, "How do you know it's bad luck?"

Sure enough, the next night the horse came back to his familiar corral . . . leading twelve wild stallions with him! . . . The neighbors heard the good news and came chattering to the farmer, "Oh, you have thirteen horses! What good luck!"

And the old Chinese answered, "How do you know that's good luck?"

A few days later his son broke his leg falling off one of the new horses and, once again the neighbors tried to console him on his bad luck.

And the wise father answered again, "How do you know it's bad luck?"

Sure enough, a few days later a Chinese warlord came through town and conscripted every able-bodied young man, taking them off to war, never to return again. But the young man was saved because of his broken leg.

Don't make assumptions based upon your narrow frame of reference until all the facts are in. The man to whom Schuller referred was the epitome of the pragmatist: he made no judgments upon events. He accepted them and let the events move to their inevitable conclusions. To conclude that the things that happened were "good luck" or "bad luck" required him to make assumptions that he was unwilling to make. He acted and waited.

So too, after an interview, you should not make evaluative judgments because they will be based upon assumptions that will have no basis in fact. How can you know whether you had a "good" or a "bad" interview? How do you know whether you made a "good" or a "bad" impression?

You waste your time by making such judgments. You are in the worst possible position to evaluate your performance. In the first place, you certainly are not able to make an objective appraisal. Second, you don't know what the specifications for the position are. Third, you can't possibly put yourself inside the head of the interviewer to determine the feeling she got from you.

Finally, what good will it do for you to make some kind of a judgment on how the interviewer thought you did? You can't go back and redo the interview. You can't change what's happened.

I once had an interview with a man for a position with a client of mine. I came away from the interview thinking that he was probably the worst interviewee I had seen in months. The next day the executive search agent who had set up the interview called for my response, and I told him that I wasn't interested in pursuing the matter further. He expressed great surprise: "When I talked with the applicant he was jubilant. He felt that he had come across well and that you had been very favorably impressed!" All that applicant did was to delude himself and build himself up for a great letdown. He had apparently made some very basic erroneous assumptions about me and my reaction, and had walked away from the interview thinking that he was very close to receiving a job offer.

All of us wonder about how we did in an interview, but wondering serves no purpose. You waste your time and you can either build yourself up for a great letdown or you can worry yourself into a state of acute depression. Wait until you discover what the interviewer's judgment on you has been before you evaluate the interview. If she rejects you, then you can gain from reviewing the interview objectively to determine what happened so that you can better prepare for the interviews in the future. If she asks you to a follow-up interview or makes you an offer, you can then bask in the glow of an interview well conducted without the possibility of being cruelly let down by believing in a false assumption.

Don't be intimidated by your competition

Inevitably, during the course of the interviewing process you will see other candidates and they will impress you. They will be good looking, well-dressed, charming, and sophisticated, and you'll assume you don't have a chance. You will feel a failure immediately. You'll wonder, what's the use? This other person has it all wrapped up.

Don't assume yourself into a position where you are intimidated by style rather than essence. When I was preparing my interview service, I videotaped interviews with three people as samples. One of the interviewees was an experienced, outgoing person who had style. Another was sort of average, and the third was a shy and retiring introvert.

In my own mind I rated them with the extrovert on top and the introvert capable of impressing no one. After I showed the interviews to prospective clients, I asked them to rate the interviewees. To my surprise, the introvert was rated first by more clients than the extrovert. They felt that the introvert's personality was more amenable to their type of operation. The extrovert came on too strong and they felt that he would be difficult to get along with.

Time and again interviewees have told me that they felt their interview was poor, but later have received more offers than the seeming "superstars."

Interviewers are rarely misled by style as a substitute for substance. They are looking for a personality that will fit in with their operation. A hail-fellow-well-met may be a smash at a party, but as a candidate for a job, he might not have the advantage that his sophistication may project.

Think positively

There is, however, one assumption that the wise interviewee should make prior to any interview. Although most selection interviewers are not knowledgeable in the art of conducting an interview, you should assume that the interview in which you are to participate is going to be professional and that the interviewer will be well prepared. Assuming this, you will take the time to prepare yourself properly in advance, using all the many techniques that are explained in this book. If you assume the best and get the worst, you are not going to be hurt. But, if you assume something less than the best and get the best, you're going to be at a disadvantage.

Norman Vincent Peale says in *The Power of Positive Thinking* that if you expect the best, you'll get it. Of course, that is not always the case, but the point he makes is valid as much in the converse as it is in concept: **If you think you're going to fail, you undoubtedly will.**

Two things that happened to me as a young lawyer point out the importance of attitude and expectations of success. I had recently become counsel of a large division, and I was going to have to negotiate with a potential supplier. I had heard stories about the abilities of their attorney and how smart and vicious he was. I was intimidated. I went into the meeting assuming that he knew a lot more about the problem than I did, and that he was more experienced. I just hoped that I could come out of the negotiation without making too much of a show of my ignorance.

The negotiation was the disaster I had anticipated. The other attorney was arrogant and intimidating. When I'd say something, he'd laugh snidely as if to say, "How can anyone be so dumb?" Afterward I was in a blue funk. Here was my first chance to leave a good impression and I had blown it.

A few weeks later I had to fly East with another negotiating team. I was told that the people with whom I would be negotiating were very nice and easy to get along with. I had no fears.

It turned out that they were not "nice." In fact, they were tougher and more knowledgeable than those in the first negotiation. But I went in confidently and unworried. I locked horns with them on several key points and emerged unscathed and victorious on each. The word got back to management that I was a tiger, and my reputation was made.

Later I met the lawyer who had so intimidated me in my first negotiation. By this time I had built confidence in myself and didn't make any assumptions about his superiority. It turned out that he was all show and no substance. When I didn't let him intimidate me and didn't assume failure, he caused me no problems.

Bad assumptions can so intimidate you that you can be defeated before the fray begins. The only cure is to prepare as best you can and have the confidence that you can handle anything that arises. Don't compare yourself with other candidates, because you don't know what the interviewer is looking for. Be yourself. It's just as likely that the interviewer is looking for you as it is that he's looking for someone completely different. If he is looking for someone completely different, you wouldn't be happy in the job in any event, so it's better to find that out.

CHECKLIST

★ A bold assertion you make can be met with an illogical reaction by the interviewer.

★ You can't discover an interviewer's quality and makeup in a short interview.

★ If you make a negative impression early with an assertion based on false assumption, you will have a very difficult time reversing the impression.

★ Closely observe the interviewer and be sensitive to her reactions.

★ Observe the interviewer's body language and react accordingly.

★ If you perceive hints you aren't being well received, stop what you're doing that may be causing the negative reaction.

★ Don't draw conclusions after the interview ends about how well or how poorly you did.

★ Don't be intimidated by your competition.

★ Think positively.

★ Don't key your performance to false assumptions.

★ Assume that you are going to be exposed to a sophisticated, professional interview technique.

★ Assume every question is asked for a reason that is job connected.

★ Assume that everyone with whom you speak before an offer or rejection is made is making a judgment of you.

HONESTY

*Honesty in an interview is made up of
three elements*: truth, consistency, and candor.

Truth

There comes a time in every interview when you will be
tempted to exaggerate your accomplishments. The interviewer (and in this chapter, let's assume the interviewer is
a man) may ask you how much money you're making, and
you may decide to add a couple of thousand dollars a year
to your actual earnings. Or he may ask you where you fin-

ished in your college class, and you may think there's little difference between the top third and the top quarter.

When you feel this temptation—and it strikes everyone, no matter how honest—remember this rule: WHEN IN DOUBT, TELL THE TRUTH! Sir Walter Scott said it years ago in iambic tetrameter:

> Oh, what a tangled web we weave,
> When first we practice to deceive!

If you lie, and that's what an exaggeration is, it may haunt you for the rest of your days. A lie is a terrible cancer that, undiscovered, can plague you with fear of discovery. Once discovered, it can destroy your credibility forever. If you are caught lying in the interview or on your résumé, the interviewer can logically assume that you will continue to lie on the job. Since no employer wants employees who cannot be trusted, you may be eliminated immediately. Even if you are not caught, what could be a worse way to start a relationship than to build it on the foundation of a lie?

It has been estimated that 22 percent of résumés contain outright lies. In one extreme case a professor at a major American university was found to have used false identities to join six other college faculties in the previous four years. Caught, he was charged with twenty-seven counts of forgery, theft by deception, false swearing, and tampering with official documents.

The Thomas Brown affair

I am as fascinated as the next person by stories of grand deceptions and imposters who have succeeded. The reality of it, though, is that sooner or later, a web of lies will almost certainly break down. Here's a classic example:

A young man to whom I shall refer to as Thomas Brown (not his real name nor any of his aliases) applied to Harvard Law School and was admitted. His application listed a degree from Tulane University. Three years later, Harvard discovered that this was false and forced Brown to withdraw from the university.

Two years later Brown was admitted to Harvard Law School again, under a different name. This time he claimed to be a graduate of Louisiana State University. He obtained loans of $2,500, the maximum amount a student may borrow.

Law school is a three-year program, and traditionally students spend the summer between their second and third years as clerks in law firms. Brown, who told the interviewing firms that he had straight A's, that he had been a football player at LSU, and that he had spent a year at Oxford, received offers from two of the largest law firms in Los Angeles, as well as invitations for follow-up interviews from major firms in other areas of the country.

Brown knew how to play his role. He wore a beard "to make him look older" (he was thirty-one at the time, claiming twenty-four), always dressed in a suit, drove a Mercedes, and dropped names judiciously. He gave the impression of wealth and would casually mention he was flying to Brazil one weekend, another far-off place the next.

He was undone while interviewing with a major New York firm. One of the partners had attended LSU and did not remember Brown playing football. An inquiry caused his house of cards to tumble. He ended up facing civil and criminal charges. As a tag line to the tawdry story, it was later discovered that Brown's wife, who was a student in the Harvard Business School, had credentials every bit as false as her husband's.

I strongly recommend against any kind of intentional deception. Eventually one of the threads will break and they'll find out you didn't play football at LSU or spend a year at Oxford or graduate from Tulane or get all A's. Then you will have invested years for naught, in addition to having your reputation ruined.

You don't know how much the interviewer knows

Few interviewees would consider lying on such a grand scale as Thomas Brown, but probably all of us would succumb to the temptation to do a little "puffing." And a little of this is acceptable—expected, in fact. Interviewers know that interviewees want to present themselves in the best possible light, and recognize that a certain amount of image enhancement will take place with interviewees exaggerating their accomplishments or down-playing their failures.

There is a fine line between embellishment and misrepresentation of facts, though, and you never want to be found on the wrong side of the line. Keep in mind that the interviewer may know much more about you than you realize. To repeat the basic rule, when in doubt, tell the truth.

A colleague of mine recommended a friend to me for a position with a client for whom I was interviewing. He told me that his friend was dissatisfied with his present job. He was making less than $20,000 per year and was looking for a higher paying position. I met with the friend and after an hour's amiable conversation I gently probed areas I felt were important and casually asked how much money he was making. He told me that he was making "around $35,000." Of course, he had no way of knowing that I knew better.

Suddenly the tenor of the interview changed. Within the space of a few moments, a metamorphosis occurred in him. The cocoon fell from this fellow and different colors shone through. Whatever subject I broached was followed by a dogmatic diatribe defending his view, which was absolute. There was no moderation in his tone, no conversational amenity. He was a completely different person.

How much of this was an attitude that was there but that I didn't perceive, and how much was caused by his lie, I can't say. But my opinion of him changed instantly. Thinking of it later, I traced this to two causes. First was the unacceptability of his lie. Second was the personality change. Did I see him with different eyes, or did his knowledge of his lie make him change? That's the danger in lying. You never know the knowledge of the person to whom you are lying; you don't know the sources available to him to check out your stories; and you are unaware of the effects that the lie has on you, and your subsequent performance!

A reader from New York writes about a problem of an opposite sort: how to downplay credentials without really lying.

We hear a lot about fictitious degrees and other credentials. My problem is the opposite—I want to *hide* some of my degrees and jobs and downplay my age. Let me explain. My old résumé showed three bachelor's degrees and a caseworker job. Yes, I did change my mind several times. However, I am now an accountant and sure about it. I started work on my accounting degree in 1974, so in one way or another have been connected with accounting for fifteen years. My old résumé posed two problems:

A. Interviewers invariably say something like "Why did you change fields so many times?" The answer is that I wasn't exposed to accounting and had no idea that would be my field. Also, I thought that showing my caseworker job on my résumé would *help me*—showing that I have *people* skills as well as *number skills*. However, I believe that, instead, the three degrees and the caseworker job just make me look wishy-washy.

B. I am forty-five years old, but look about thirty. While I can't prove age discrimination, I strongly suspect it exists. I don't have the time, money, or inclination to fight it—I just want a job. However, I believe that I can fight it my own way—through omissions on my résumé.

My feeling is this: I am generally an honest person. I am applying for positions for which I feel I qualify. I am in excellent health and physical condition. Therefore, why should I put something on my résumé that is irrelevant and that could hurt me? After all, I could also put down grade school, high school, Girl Scouts, babysitting and other teenage activities. Where do you draw the line?

If anybody subsequently asks me about these omissions, I am prepared to say, "I feel it was too long ago and not relevant."

I was laid off from my last paid job where I had worked four years, due to lack of work. I was not replaced. I had always had an itch to start my own practice, but had been afraid to quit my job to do it. So I figured as long as I was laid off, this was the time to try to start my own practice.

Although I have quite a few individual tax clients and have some businesses, I have to admit the business is a failure. I think the only way I could make a go of it would be to buy out or merge with another practice. I am, for the most part, being supported by my husband's salary, and am now actively seeking employment.

My question is this: Should I tell interviewers I left to start my own business, or should I say I was laid off, and then decided to start my own business?

If I say I left to start my own business, an interviewer might think I lacked common sense to quit a secure job for a business that didn't prove successful. He also might think I am wishy-washy, not giving myself enough time for success, as it usually takes three years to establish a practice.

If I say I was laid off, it might be more understandable why after just one year, I decided to re-enter the job market. On the other hand, "laid off" may have a stigma.

This reader needs to realize that the purpose of a résumé is to get an interview, not to get a job. Once the résumé gets you in the door for the interview, it's up to you to continue on and the résumé becomes much less important. So the only time you have to worry about deceptive omissions in your résumé is when the deception is of something that would *substantively* affect the interviewer's evaluation of you. Having too many degrees is not such a thing; having spent ten years in San Quentin for rape is. If it is her opinion that she is the victim of age discrimination and that she can fight it by changing her résumé, then I think she should and wouldn't worry about such omissions. You want to be honest, but you don't want to roll up your sleeves to show your interviewer your newest wart!

Part of the reader's problem is a question of semantics and phrasing her answer in the best possible light. I don't like the stigma of the words "laid off," either. Her *job* was terminated. While this might be a fine distinction (since the result is the same) she should have explained her situation more fully than just saying she was "laid off." She should have explained that she had a good job and was doing good work and that her employer was happy with her but that there just wasn't enough work for him to have someone else working for him. That sounds better then just saying she was "laid off," and has the added virtue of being the truth.

Further, if I were she, I wouldn't say that I left to start my own business, because it's not true and the reason she found herself on her own was not something that would be a negative. Had she slugged her boss in the nose and lost her job because of that, then she would have had something to worry about in trying to explain it in the best light, but what happened to her is not a negative; it just has to be fully explained when the question is raised.

Differing interpretations

Most occurrences are subject to different interpretations.

What must be distinguished is the intentional misrepresentation of an established fact from the embellishment of the interpretation of the situation.

Examples of misrepresentation are saying you made more money than you actually did, misrepresenting time periods in your résumé, or saying you finished higher in your graduating class than you actually did. If you misrepresent a verifiable fact that is not subject to interpretation and it is discovered, the interview process might end right there, or, if you have already been hired, you may find your job terminated.

But if the question calls for an interpretation, you can shade your answer so that you show up to your best advantage without actually lying. After I gave a lecture at a Western university, a student came up to me with a real problem. He was ranked third in his law school class, but he had not yet received an offer, despite the fact that the recruiting season was almost over. He seemed to me to be eager, intelligent, and personable, so I asked him what he thought was behind his lack of success. He said it might be because he had been invited to try out for the *Law Review* and had declined and that the interviewers didn't like this. His explanation to interviewers was that the *Review* took a lot of time, and he didn't want to sacrifice his social life for all that work.

If I ever heard an answer calculated to turn off a prospective employer, that was it. I asked him if he spent all his time playing and he responded, somewhat indignantly, that he did not. He spent most of his time studying, and what little leisure time he did have he needed to use just for leisure, not further legal work on the *Review*. I asked him if he had gone into this much detail when interviewers asked him his reasons for not applying for the *Review* and he said that he had not.

I suggested to him that he tell the truth, but that it be the complete truth, not just a short lazy truth. By shortchanging his answer he had left the impression that he didn't like hard work. By adding a few more details he could leave a completely different impression, that of someone who worked hard, but was mature enough to realize that in order to work hard he needed leisure time to recharge his batteries.

The interviewer was asking for an explanation why he did not try out for the *Review*. When asked for such an opinion, the interviewee should answer the question to his best advantage which can result in the interviewer's evaluating him on the whole interview and not on one very bad answer that had a "halo" effect. (For more on the halo effect, see chapter 14.)

Consistency

Inconsistency is a fault that can be almost as damaging as lying. You must take great care to be consistent in your interviews, especially in screening interviews when you are faced with trained personnel officers whose goal is to uncover the facts.

Remember, screening interviewers are looking for reasons to reject you. They are looking for inconsistencies on your résumé and in what you say. If they get a glimmer of something wrong, they may ask the same question over and over in different ways to test what you have claimed. If you have told the truth, you generally have nothing to fear in an interrogation like this. But if you have misrepresented something, or if you have hedged an answer to show yourself in the best light, you must be very careful that each time you discuss that topic you say the same thing. If you once vary from what you have said before, you may either be rejected for that or you may have to justify the variance.

The selection interviewer is also looking for inconsistencies, but not with the same fervor that a screening interviewer may. But if he gets a red flag to one of his questions, beware. If you claim some accomplishment that he feels is beyond you, he may go into the subject in depth and probe the area to determine exactly what you did and how much you participated in the event.

For example, if I were interviewing the student who didn't try out for the *Review* and he told me that he wanted to devote all the time he could to his studies, I would let some time pass and then question him on his outside interests. If I then discovered that he played intramural sports, never missed a first-run movie, went to all the football and basketball games, and dated a different woman every night, I'd conclude that his reason for not trying out for the Review was inconsistent with his actions.

Candor

The third element of honesty is candor. As a rule, interviewees look upon a selection interview as a one-way street. On the one side sits the interviewer who is picking a person to fill an available position. On the other side is the interviewee who is applying for the position.

But it works both ways. You as applicant are also an interviewer seeking to find out if the position is right for you. If something bothers you about the position for which you are interviewing, you should be candid about your doubt and express it to the interviewer. I counseled a man once who told me that he had turned down an attractive job offer because the interviewer, the vice president to whom he would report, was abrasive with a subordinate. He felt that he would not react well if he were treated in a similar manner. I asked if he had discussed the problem with the vice president, and he replied that he had not. He had simply declined the offer. He felt badly about it because what he knew about the position stimulated him.

You should realize that when a job is offered, it is a compliment. The employer is saying, "I like you and I think you can do a good job. I am so confident of this that I'm willing to pay you to come and work for me." When a compliment is paid, it should be treated with respect. If for some reason you decide to reject the job offer you owe it to both yourself and to the offerer to state the reasons for the rejection. First, it is courteous. Second, and more important, as far as you are concerned, the offerer may wish to resolve the problems you have with the job by making it more palatable.

The person I was counseling had a fear that the vice president would be difficult to work with. He made this judgment on the basis of one incident and didn't give the man another chance. It's possible that his interviewer had just been released from the hospital, or a close relative had died, or he had lost a lot of money in the stock market, or the subordinate could have been completely incompetent, or he could have had some other disappointment about which the interviewee knew nothing. If he doesn't raise the point, he isn't getting the most out of his interview. He should try and get as much information as he can.

Had he turned down the position by saying something like: "I appreciate the offer, but frankly I am very concerned about how you and I would work together. . . . I consider myself a professional and, as a result, feel that I am due professional respect and courtesy. . . . The way you spoke to Mr. Smith troubled me . . . " He would have given the interviewer an opportunity to face the interviewee's main objection to the job and at least explain his actions.

Remember the advice previously given on assumptions. Don't base your decision on unqueried assumptions that may be erroneous. Be as certain as you can that your assumption is based on fact. You can do this by being candid and bringing your assumptions out into the open. If you think the job is an attractive one but you have grave doubts because of something about which you haven't spoken, bring it up and discuss it with the interviewer prior to making your decision.

One executive I knew made a terrible career mistake because he was not candid during the interview process. A reputable company had been trying to find a new vice president of finance. It had been interviewing for over a year to fill a vacancy that had had several occupants the preceding two years. Obviously something was wrong.

The executive went to the interview, despite severe misgivings. He met the top management and was impressed. Still his doubts nagged.

He was made an offer that was beyond his wildest dreams: a large salary, a Lincoln Continental, bonus, profit sharing, everything he had ever wanted. On the debit side was that he knew that the three people in the job before him had only stayed a few months before leaving. He also knew that the company had had the vacancy for more than a year. This troubled him, but he feared to bring it up.

Analyzing the situation later, he knew that his fear had two bases. First, he felt that a question about the turnover might offend the interviewer and cost him an offer. Second, he feared that the answer might cause him to have to reject an offer he wanted. So he didn't broach the subject, took the job, and immediately found himself in the eye of a storm.

Apparently there were shenanigans with one of the recently acquired divisions that could subject the company to shareholders' derivative suits and the officers involved to extensive liability. Each of his predecessors had apparently discovered the problem quickly and resigned rather than become embroiled in such a dangerous situation.

My friend had large personal expenses, and couldn't afford to quit. His résumé had so many job changes that he felt he couldn't put his name out on the street, so he had to try to survive without participating in the problem and thereby becoming an accomplice.

He was stuck in a miserable situation for two years before an offer appeared at a much smaller company for much less money. He grabbed it without looking back.

Had he been candid and expressed his doubts, he could have discovered the problem prior to taking the job. Of course, the company wouldn't have admitted such a thing to a job candidate, but he could have listened to their explanation and then told them he wanted to talk to the men who had held the position previously. That most probably would have either terminated the company's consideration of him, or he would have discovered from his predecessors that the situation was sticky.

It's never wise to accept or reject an offer if you have unexpressed doubts about something. Bring them out into the open. They may be unfounded, and you will be able to start your new position with a clear mind. Or they may have foundation, in which case you're better off knowing about it and not proceeding further (or proceeding further with full knowledge of what you're getting into). In either case, you're much better off by being candid and expressing your doubts than keeping them to yourself.

Evasiveness

Reader Steven Shore, of Columbia, Maryland, writes:

I've been asked in interviews if I have ever done X. Of course the interviewer has neither the interest nor the ability to take us both back in time, but is asking the question because he or she has made two implicit assumptions: that X is perceived as an essential skill in the job in question; and that the only way the candidate can actually perform X in the job is by having successfully performed X in the past.

This type of question, in my opinion, allows only three basic answers: (1) "Yes, I have done X at_____; this resulted in $_____ of new product or service growth or $_____ of cost savings; (2) "No, I haven't done X. However, I have successfully done Y, which resulted in [proceed as in (1) above]; (3) "No, I haven't done X."

I wish we lived in a world where answer #2 would be credibly received, but this is usually not the case. So under certain conditions, i.e., if I believe that I can accomplish X in the job in question, I will give answer #1.

I would always prefer to give an honest answer. However, in more than one instance I have perceived that honesty really wasn't expected or appreciated by the interviewer, that in giving an honest answer to a question I had removed myself from consideration for a position I could function effectively in, and in an environment where I'd fit in quite well.

Mr. Shore's letter goes right to the heart of the matter, and the problem may be resolved in a way that is not dishonest. Very few questions ask strictly for facts. If someone asks you straight out if you've ever done X and you haven't and don't want to admit it, answer to your best advantage. You can answer as if you think they've asked you if you're *familiar* with X or if you *think* you could do X, or how you would *approach* X if given the opportunity. What interviewees often fail to realize is that an interview is not a script. There aren't written questions and answers to which the interviewer can later refer. It's a dialogue and generally the interviewer is just trying to get the interviewee to talk.

Further, if you misinterpret the question (intentionally or unintentionally) the interviewer might immediately recognize that you're not answering the question he asked as specifically as he asked it. It's unlikely that he'll reask the question because (1) it can be insulting to the interviewee, and (2) he might like your answer and not want to get another. Interviewers are not prosecuting attorneys, and generally don't bore in until they get the specific answer to the specific question they asked. More probably he'll just go on to other subjects and not repeat the question. Interviewers are as lazy as everyone else and might not want to exert the effort to try to force you to answer the question when you've already talked on the subject for awhile. Another, depending on how well you've vamped, is the time constraints of the interview. He might just want to go on to other things.

If you haven't done X and don't want to admit it, it's not dishonest to answer the question by talking about something else. The interviewer won't know if you are being evasive or misheard the question, or if he didn't ask the question properly. If he's really interested in the specific answer to the question, he'll ask it again, and then you don't have much choice but to answer it. If he's not, then answering a different question than what was asked has accomplished your purpose of not admitting that you haven't done X without lying about it. Whether or not your evasiveness has been noticed is something you might never find out.

CHECKLIST

★ Honesty consists of truth, consistency, and candor.

★ When in doubt, tell the truth.

★ An undiscovered lie will haunt you.

★ A discovered lie can destroy your credibility forever.

★ An employer does not want someone working for him whom he cannot trust.

★ Failure to tell the truth reveals a character trait that cannot be remedied.

★ Remember that you have no way of knowing how much the interviewer knows.

★ A lie can change your personality as your guilty knowledge of it affects your performance.

★ Distinguish between a question calling for fact and one calling for an opinion.

★ Always answer questions calling for your opinion to your best advantage.

★ Inconsistency can lead to an inference of a lack of honesty.

★ Be candid about your doubts and bring them up to the interviewer.

★ A job offer is a compliment, and you owe the interviewer the courtesy of being candid.

★ Don't base your decision on unqueried assumptions.

CONFIDENCE, NERVOUSNESS, AND RELAXATION

*Believe in yourself. Even if you don't believe in yourself, if
you make the interviewer think that you do, you'll be
on the right track.*

At a youthful twenty-five, Irving Thalberg was the head of production at MGM. It was the early twenties, and Hollywood was in its ascendancy. Thalberg's pictures were enormously successful and profitable, and it was said that "Thalberg is always right." As one person described it, Thalberg exhibited "a glacial calm" when confronted with the decisions involving millions of dollars he had to make day after day. Did Irving Thalberg have confidence in himself? Did he ever doubt his judgment? This is what he confided to F. Scott Fitzgerald when he was at the height of his power:

> Supposing there's got to be a road through the mountain and ... there seems to be a half-dozen possible roads ... each one of which, so far as you can determine, is as good as the other. Now suppose you happen to be the top man, there's a point where you don't exercise the faculty of judgment in the ordinary way, but simply the faculty of arbitrary decision. You say, "Well, I think we will put the road there," and you trace it with your finger and you know in your secret heart, and no one else knows, that you have no reason for putting the road there rather than in several other different courses, but you're the only person who knows that you don't know why you're doing it and you've got to stick to that and you've got to pretend that you know that you did it for specific reasons, even though you're utterly assailed by doubts at times as to the wisdom of your decision, because all these other possible decisions keep echoing in your ear. But when you're planning a new enterprise on a grand scale, the people under you mustn't ever know or guess that you're in doubt, because they've all got to have something to look up to and they mustn't ever dream that you're in doubt about any decision.

Everyone has doubts. Irving Thalberg had them. Julius Caesar had them. We all have them. But keep them hidden, at least in an interview. This is one time when you must exude confidence in who you are and what you say.

There are many ways to develop the appearance of confidence. Success breeds it. If you are offered some jobs, you'll begin to think that you're a pretty hot item, and you will enter interviews exuding it. But if you aren't made a lot of offers, **you can't let rejection erode your confidence in yourself.**

The subject of the interview is you

In developing confidence, you must recognize the things that tend to make you lack it. It is fear of the unknown that attacks and weakens your resolve. But there should be no such fear in being interviewed. First of all, an interview is centered on the subject you know best: yourself. The interview is much more of an unknown for the interviewer (and for this chapter let's assume the interviewer is a woman). Most likely, all she knows about you is what is on your résumé.

If you have done your preparation as described in Chapter 2, you'll know a good deal about the company and you might even know something about the interviewer if you've been diligent enough to do some detective work. You also know that she is probably tired and perhaps bored. She's interviewed many people and gone through this routine time and again, asking the same questions and getting the same responses. She doesn't know what you're going to say, but you know what you want to say. So there is no reason for you not to feel confident. You're better prepared than the interviewer is. You know far more about the subject under discussion than she does. The interview is yours.

If you've done your homework and are prepared for the interview, you have nothing to fear. Basically the interviewer is going to ask you questions about yourself. What in the world could you know better than yourself? She can't ask a question that will stump you because she will limit herself to questions about your background and your ideas.

Appendix A contains three lists of questions that might be thrown at you in an interview. It's unlikely that an interviewer will come up with a question that is not at least touched upon in these lists. So go into the interview confident that she's not going to throw something at you from left field.

Nervousness

Most interviewers expect a certain amount of nervousness on the part of those interviewing for lower-level positions. Certainly a campus interviewer would think it normal that a student who has been through very few interviews and has never held a full-time job would be nervous. Sweaty palms and nervous speech would be understandable.

But if a person is being interviewed by the executive committee of a large corporation for the position as president of the corporation, nervousness would undoubtedly make a very poor impression. A candidate for a position at a high level is expected to be confident. The exhibition of nervousness through a sweaty palm or forehead or a nervous tic would be an indication of a lack of confidence and would be noted. An interviewer may not consciously exclude the candidate for exhibiting such a human weakness, but the impression would almost certainly lead to a negative judgment.

Sweaty palms

Almost without exception, interviewers state that they overlook sweaty palms because they expect a certain amount of nervousness. The only exception to this rule is the situation where they are interviewing people for jobs that require a person with a great deal of self-confidence, such as a corporate executive, or a position in sales, promotions, or public relations.

But some interviewers are honest enough to admit that sweaty palms can be a powerful factor in rejection. Leonard Zunin, in *Contact: The First Four Minutes*, states that one personnel director told him, "Regardless of the qualifications of a man he interviews, 'If his handshake is weak and clammy, he's out.'" Zunin goes on to comment: "Such reaction to body language is probably far more prevalent than we realize, as others assume many things about our glance, stance, or advance."

An honest interviewer will candidly admit that a sweaty palm makes their skin crawl. Even though they may recognize it as a normal sign of nervousness, it creates a less-than-favorable initial impression. Dr. Carlotta Mellon, who was Appointments Assistant to former California governor Edmund G. Brown, Jr., admits, "I react negatively to sweaty palms. People should try not to be so nervous. . . . They should probably have a handkerchief in hand to wipe their hands. . . . I think that sweaty palms convey a lack of confidence."

The general counsel of a major New York Stock Exchange corporation once told me of an interviewee who was so concerned about his sweaty palms that just before entering the interview, he went to wash his hands. Unfortunately he didn't dry them sufficiently, and when they shook hands, the general counsel felt cold moisture that he said "made me cringe."

No one would refuse to make an offer to a superstar because of sweaty palms, but why start out an interview doing something that makes your interviewer cringe? It doesn't matter whether the moisture comes from nervous perspiration or insufficiently dried clean hands. Your first contact should be a positive one, and you should ensure that your hands are dry.

If you're nervous, no matter how many times you wash your hands or dry them off with a handkerchief, they'll still sweat. One method to reduce the moisture is to sit with your palms exposed while you wait to be called into the interview. If you have your palms covered, whether they are in your lap or in your pockets, the heat will increase the sweating. If you allow the air to get at them, the moisture will be kept to a minimum. I have found that if I sit with my hands dangling down at my sides or sit with my palms in my lap but facing upward, sweaty palms cease to be a problem. These positions may feel awkward, but your interviewer isn't going to see you waiting, and what's important is that you not give her a wet hand when she offers hers to you.

How others handle nervousness

Different people deal with nervousness in ways that may seem uncommon, but work for them. Actor-director Gene Wilder says that he actually screams aloud to relieve tension and nervousness. To relieve tension before his performances, the late Sir Laurence Olivier used to utter the most vile words in the English language to the audience, although not so loud that they could hear. One prizefighter said, after the end of his career, that if he could have screamed anything at the spectators before his matches, just so it was screamed aloud, he would have been a champion.

If you analyze nervousness, its causes and effects, you will recognize that it is a symptom of something else. Two successful men with similar jobs told how they handle nervous feelings:

As chairman of the board of Whittaker Corporation, Joseph F. Alibrandi had a grueling work schedule and a large load of responsibilities. He disdained nervousness and ways to combat it. "I don't look at the world that way," he said. "Sure, I get nervous, but that's part of doing it. See, the getting nervous is a symptom of the challenge of the problem. For me to sit back and work on curing the symptom just doesn't accomplish anything. What I've got to do is, there's something to be done and I've got to focus on getting that thing done. If there's nervousness as a symptom and perspiration and wet palms or whatever it is, that's fine, I'm not going to deal with those. They're just symptoms. I don't think there's a guy in the world who's not scared or what have you. I don't believe in Valium and all the other baloney. The problem is the problem and it's not going to change. If you've decided you've done everything you can do to optimize your probability to succeed, then you just jump in and do it."

The former president of another major corporation looks at it this way. "My experience is that if you prepare yourself properly, you really don't have the time or inclination for the fright symptoms to appear.

"Since we're still dealing with human beings and there will be considerable gaps in their preparation, those things do occur. Among the things that I have found of some use is just before you come into the interview, give yourself some physical stress, even if it's only to the point of trying to run in place, or if you don't want to appear to be out of breath, do some isometrics of one sort or another. But do

118

concentrate on the physical aspects, rather than the mental aspects just before an interview. Just point out to yourself that any time you spend any of your own personal energy on the symptoms, you're just wasting preparation that you should have.

"It's rather like trying to prepare for a classroom performance. There are all sorts of ways in which you can blow it. You can forget a half-hour of material that you have stored up in your head, which can certainly be done that night. You're much better off to say, 'Well, that's one circumstance about which there's very little control. My job here is to perform in as forceful a fashion to be of service to other people as possible.' You don't make yourself of service to somebody else if you're not relaxed, if you're not sensitive to other people's needs."

How to combat sleeplessness

Nervousness attacks at different times, not just immediately prior to entering the interview room. Many people are so tense about an upcoming interview that they are unable to sleep the night before, tossing and turning and looking at the clock every ten or fifteen minutes.

Here are some suggestions for alleviating sleeplessness when the insomnia is caused by worry or tension.

1. **Muscular relaxation.** When you are worried about something, your mind continues to function and tenses the muscles. But you will not be able to sleep until you can relax your muscles. Dr. Walter Alvarez, the noted medical writer, suggests taking a warm bath if you feel that your body is tense. The heat tends to relax your muscles and make you drowsy.

2. **Food or drink.** Often people get sleepy after they eat. The physiological explanation may be that the blood rushes to your stomach to aid in the digestive process. Whatever the reason, sometimes a hot meal—or even a warm glass of milk—can cause drowsiness.

3. **Alcohol.** Although this is reputed to be the first step on the road to alcoholism, many people find that a glass of wine or beer before retiring allows them to relax and get to sleep quickly, but the qual-

ity of alcohol induced sleep may be counter-productive because it can disrupt your sleep during the night.

4. **Drugs.** Tranquilizers such as Valium and Librium are much in vogue as sleeping pills. Any drugs such as these should not be taken unless a doctor has prescribed it. Even then, sometimes the side effects are worse than the cure. **It is not at all unusual for a tranquilizer to cause drowsiness the next morning and a lethargy that is difficult to shake quickly.** Unless you are experienced in taking such drugs, the night before a big interview is not the time to experiment just for the sake of getting to sleep. If you do ask your doctor for such a drug and plan on using it to ensure a good night's sleep before an interview, try it out a few nights before your interview so you know how it will affect you the next morning.

   Even if you take a pill to get to sleep and do actually sleep, there's no assurance that it will do you a bit of good. Richard M. Coleman, who was co-director of the Sleep Disorder Clinic at Stanford University, states that "people who take the pill at night are actually **sleepier** in the daytime than if they'd just stayed up all night or had a bad night of sleep **without** the pill."

Coleman gives several rules for developing good sleep habits. You should follow them before interviews about which you are nervous:

1. Have a regular schedule.

2. The sleep environment should be quiet and completely dark.

3. Avoid alcohol after dinner.

4. Try to place some limit on the amount of coffee you drink. If you drink coffee in the daytime, you probably should limit it to the morning hours. The more coffee you take, the more your brain needs that amount just to get to its basic level of arousal.

5. Exercise helps you sleep. It is best performed in the late afternoon between 4 and 6, if you plan to go to bed around 11. If you exercise too soon before going to bed, it seems to disturb sleep.

6. Plan your time before you go to bed. You should try to wind down a little bit. If you came home at your normal bedtime, go to sleep a little later that night. Take the time to unwind, not with alcohol, but just relax and talk to someone or watch television and go to bed a little bit later. Then try to get up at the normal time the next morning.

Milton in *Paradise Lost* said, "The mind in its own place, and in itself, can make a Heaven of Hell and a Hell of Heaven." Shakespeare's Caesar said, "Cowards die many times before their deaths; the valiant never taste of death but once."

Both were making the same point. Worry avails you nothing. As I've said before, preparation is the key to combatting nervousness. If you've prepared well, you should not have to worry. An interviewer is only asking you about yourself and no one on this earth knows that subject better than you. The best way to get to sleep is to forget the interview. By the night before the interview, you have done all that it is possible for you to do. If you haven't done all that you can, you may be justified in feeling guilty, but worry isn't going to allow you to do the preparation you feel you should have done. Just forget it and let it happen.

You've got nothing to lose

Nervousness and lack of confidence are often caused by fear of losing. But what have you got to lose? People are nervous going into a job interview because they fear that they will not get an offer or be invited to return. **But they didn't have an offer before the interview. If they still don't have an offer after the interview, they are no worse off. So why worry?**

Throw caution to the wind. Look at the downside. What is the absolute worst that can happen to you? You won't get an offer. Well, right now you don't have an offer, so the downside is simply a maintenance of the status quo. That's nothing to worry about. Go into the interview forgetting about yourself. For fifteen minutes exude self-confidence. Take a chance. If you recognize that not getting that for which you hope is no disaster, you will be much looser and will try things that may work. If they don't work, you're no worse off.

When I was a young lawyer I once left a job with a law firm because I was intensely bored. After a summer of contemplation in Manhattan Beach, I decided that I wanted to work in a corporate law department. I made calls and wrote letters and finally got an interview with a vice-president and general counsel of a major airline company.

He was courteous, but at the end of the interview he said that he just didn't have enough work to justify another attorney. I returned home and wrote him a long letter volunteering to work for nothing. I told him that at that stage of my career the experience was worth more than the money. It was, truly, an outstanding letter, and I waited confidently for his reply. How could he possibly turn down such a magnanimous offer?

Well, I found out it was pretty easy for him to turn it down. He replied that he just didn't feel like he wanted to accept that responsibility. It can be crushing when someone tells you he doesn't want you to work for him for free! But I didn't let it dissuade me. I kept plugging and finally got a much better job. The point is that you've got to try. **If you can see something you want, go after it in any way you can. You can't worry about rejection, and you can't let rejection get you down on yourself.**

I didn't hang my head and hide because of his refusal to hire me. I knew that I had done all that I could to get a job I wanted. I hadn't lost anything. Before I wrote the letter I didn't have the job. Afterward I still didn't have the job but I was no worse off. I had been honest and aggressive. If you do your best, if you take your best shot and still miss, you have nothing to feel badly about. I felt exhilarated. I knew I had fought the battle.

Advice of others can hurt your confidence

Confidence is often shaken by the advice of others. They'll tell you that you can't do this and that you shouldn't do that. They'll beat you down and get you to thinking negatively.

On December 12, 1900, a dinner party was given in New York City to introduce Charles Schwab, a thirty-eight-year-old Pittsburgh steel man to the East Coast banking establishment. The kings of the financial world were present, including J. Pierpont Morgan.

The hosts of the dinner, J. Edward Simmons and Charles Steward Smith, advised Schwab that the other guests would not be receptive to a long speech and told him to keep any remarks he might wish to make to fifteen or twenty minutes.

Schwab knew what he wanted to say and he said it—for an hour and a half. And he kept his audience spellbound. After it was over, Morgan took him aside, and they conferred for another hour. The result was the formation of a steel trust that is known today as the U.S. Steel Corporation.

Had Schwab changed his mind in accordance with the advice given him by his hosts, he would not have achieved the enormous success that was his. He had the strength of character and confidence in himself to do what he had planned to do in spite of the warnings of his generous hosts.

Don't look back

Eddie Rickenbacker was exposed to this attitude after he got the job with Frayer. He progressed to mechanic and, after building a racing car, it was entered in the Vanderbilt Cup, an elimination race among twelve American cars to determine the five American entrants. As mechanic, Rickenbacker rode in the car with Frayer, who was the driver.

Shortly after the elimination race began, the car developed engine trouble and had to drop out of the race. Frayer sat in the car for a long moment and then said simply, "We're through."

Rickenbacker was deeply impressed. He knew that an entire year of hard work had gone into preparation for entering the car in the Vanderbilt Cup and the car hadn't even survived the elimination race. Rickenbacker said, "I never forgot it. Gradually, over the years, the significance of that remark sank in, and I drew inspiration from it. To spell it out: TRY LIKE HELL TO WIN, BUT DON'T CRY IF YOU LOSE."

Rejection may lead to a job

Rickenbacker's inspiration should be the motto for every interviewee. Interviewing is a terrible shock to the ego because it results in so many rejections. Even outstanding candidates will be rejected by the vast majority of interviewers. The odds in interviewing are long. If you receive favorable attention in one interview out of ten, you are doing well. That means that you must come to grips with rejection nine times out of ten attempts. You've got to keep your head high and find ways to compensate for the beating your ego must take.

But you never know where a rejection will lead. When I was in law school, many classmates wanted to work in Europe for the summer, as did I, but nobody did anything about it but dream. Then one day, I wrote letters to thirty law firms throughout Europe asking for a summer job. A month later some replies started dribbling in, mostly one-line letters of rejection. One man, Peter Crane, a London solicitor, was different. He wrote me a three-page letter telling me what it was like practicing law in London. He closed with a rejection, saying that they didn't hire summer clerks from America.

I wrote him a thank-you letter. I felt that even though I had been unanimously rejected, I had learned something. But it didn't end there. Two years later I received another letter from Peter Crane saying that his firm had an opening for an American attorney and asking if I would be interested! From there I took a job that was the dream of probably every law student in America—working in a London solicitor's office!

Whenever you get down on yourself while going through the interviewing process, consider what Teddy Roosevelt had to say about trying and failing and trying again:

> It is not the critic who counts, not the man who points out how the strong man stumbled and fell, or where the doer of deeds could have done them better. The credit belongs to the man who is actually in the arena: whose face is marred by dust, sweat and blood; who strives valiantly; who errs and comes short again and again . . . who knows the great enthusiasms, the great devotions and spends himself in a worthy cause; and at the best knows in the end the triumph of high achievement; and who, at the worst,

if he fails, at least fails while daring greatly, so that his place shall never be with those cold and timid souls who know neither victory nor defeat.

Relaxation

Relaxation is as important as any of the other techniques suggested in this book. But it almost needs to be treated with an admonition because the more one tries to achieve it, the further one tends to move in the opposite direction.

This virtue is important not only in interviewing but in virtually every endeavor you undertake. Above all, relax! That's easy to say. Here you're reading this book that emphasizes how important the selection interview is, and now you're told to relax. How in God's name can you relax when so much is riding on your interview?

The answer isn't easy, but it's one that each person must determine for themselves. No matter what you try, you do it better if you're relaxed. Tennis players do much better when they're playing someone they know than when they're taking on the club champion. Suddenly their forehands are sailing into the fence, their backhands dribble off the frame, and they end up with the ball in their teeth while attempting to volley. Why? Because against their friend they are loose and aren't concerned with making mistakes. Against the club champion, mistakes are all they think about. As a result, that's what they do: make mistakes.

Timothy Gallwey in his best-selling book *The Inner Game of Tennis*, advises his readers that the way to stop thinking mistakes on the tennis court is to concentrate on minutiae, such as focusing on the seams of the ball or saying "bounce" each time the ball hits the ground and "hit" each time the ball hits the racket.

Judgments cause tension

Gallwey probes the reason why we become tense and make mistakes. **He says that it is the judgments that we make on ourselves that keep us from relaxing.**

> What I mean by judgment is the act of assigning a negative or positive value to an event. . . . What is important to see here is that neither the "goodness" nor "badness" ascribed to the event . . . is an attribute of the [event] itself. Rather, they are evaluations *added* to the event in the minds of the players according to their individual reactions.

If you apply this to your everyday life you will discover its truth. If you simply observe something, you attach no value to it and you're totally relaxed.

But why do we make judgments? It's because when we do something, we expect certain results. If we don't achieve the desired result, then we make the judgment that it was bad. If we achieve the result we wanted, then we make the judgment that it was good.

In an interview, how can we keep ourselves from making judgments and then tying ourselves up in knots when we do not achieve our artificially imposed result?

View each interview as pragmatically as possible. Sure, you have a goal. But most people mistake their goal. Most of us going into an interview are completely inwardly directed. We say, "I'm going to an interview. I hope I get an offer." Already we've imposed a result upon the event that is not only not probable; it is not justified.

You are interviewing them

Remember what was said earlier: An interview is a two-way street. Certainly they are interviewing you to see if they want to offer you a job. But you are also interviewing them to see if you want to work for them. You are going to make some decisions on them, just as they will make some decisions on you. You must approach each interview in this frame of mind. If you do, you will eliminate the prime cause for tension: your artificially imposed objective of getting an offer. You don't know if you want an offer! **Go into the interview with the objective of finding out something about them.** Tell yourself, "I want to find out what it would be like to work for this outfit. Then I'll make a decision after I've gotten the data I need and thought about it for awhile."

If you take this approach to an interview, you'll find your frame of mind before an interview changes dramatically. No longer will you be worrying about your sweaty palms or what you say when you meet the interviewer. You won't be worrying about yourself. You'll be concerned about finding out about your interviewer and his company. You'll be outwardly oriented. You won't be setting objectives for your performance and the interviewer's evaluation. You won't be making **judgments** on your own performance, so you'll be relaxed.

When you are tense and you strain, your mind blocks and you don't respond in a normal manner. Don't worry about what you're going to say and how you're going to say it. If you have a general idea of what you want to cover, let it go at that and just be ready.

Years ago, Maxwell Maltz dealt with the mysterious effects of relaxation in his book *Psycho-Cybernetics:*

> You must learn to trust your creative mechanism to do its work and not "jam it" by becoming too concerned or too anxious as to whether it will work or not, or by attempting to force it by too much conscious effort. You must **let it** work, rather than **make it** work. This trust is necessary because your creative mechanism operates below the level beneath the surface. Moreover, its nature is to operate **spontaneously** according to present need. Therefore, you have no guarantees in advance. It comes into operation as you act and as you place a demand upon it by your actions. You must not wait to act until you have proof—you must act as if it is there, and it will come through. "Do the thing and you will have the power," said Emerson.

Gallwey talks about this on the tennis court. He says that you must trust your inner self and "let it happen." If you're trying to be funny, you're not. If you're trying to be profound, you sound silly. Just relax and trust your normal reactions. An interview is, in essence, the inter-relationship between two people. Each must react to the other.

Mean Joe Greene played defensive tackle for the Super Bowl champion Pittsburgh Steelers. The first half of the 1976 football season was a bad one for him. He played subpar football and the Steelers suffered, losing several games in a row. Suddenly things turned around. Greene became the player he had been, and the Steelers, who had lost four of their first five games, won eleven in a row, allowing only twenty-eight points in their next nine games. What had caused the turnaround? "I was trying too hard not to make mistakes," Greene said. "In the past, I never gave a damn about mistakes. I used to play about 70 percent by design and 30 percent freelance. I'd take a chance now and then."

Once Greene forgot about himself and how he was performing, he resumed playing at the caliber he had achieved in the past. Thinking about what he wanted to do and worrying about mistakes caused him to make the very mistakes he was worrying about.

How to relax

Everyone must find their own method of relaxing in potentially stressful situations. Even though the interview is important, it is not Armageddon. Look upon it as an experience. Afterward, analyze how you reacted to the interviewer's questions and try to determine how she reacted to you. If you can adopt a clinical approach to what's going to happen, if you can view it as a test from which you are going to improve yourself with new knowledge and awareness, you may tend to relax.

The process of being interviewed inevitably involves a period of waiting. This is the time when the most intense nervousness attacks. Your mind is racing a mile a minute trying to remember all the things you want to say and do. You're trying to keep your hands from sweating. You want to make sure your hair is not mussed, that your clothes are neat. Your heart is beating at a faster pace than normal. Your blood pressure is probably elevated. Above all, your mind is working overtime, telling you to check all the things you've previously thought of in preparing for the interview—and adding a few more.

Since it's too late to do any more preparation, you must relax your mind. This first step is to relax physically. Close your eyes and concentrate on relaxing each muscle in your body, beginning with your toes. Once your toes are relaxed, think about your ankles, then your calves, then your knees, then your thigh muscles, then your hips. Progress to your stomach muscles, your chest. Take some deep breaths. Then relax your neck. Lay your head back.

When your body is finally in a state of relaxation, cleanse your mind. Try to think of something calming and pleasant like a waterfall or the waves at the beach or a snowcapped peak with the deep blue sky beyond.

If you concentrate on relaxing your muscles and ridding your mind of all but pleasant thoughts, you should be able to feel the tension drain from your body. Your heartbeat will slow, the sweating will diminish, your mind will cease its race.

Know when to stop preparing

In order to relax, you must at some point cease preparing for the interview. As a student I recognized this when studying for exams in law school. I would completely drop out of everything three weeks preceding exams. I stayed in my room and spent the entire time memorizing my class notes, comprising hundreds of pages. I had a strict schedule that I followed religiously.

But the day before my first exam, I put away all my notes. That day I played basketball or tennis. That night I went to a movie. Between exams I played basketball and went to movies. I did not return to my notes. I knew that I had studied enough either to know it or not. If I did not know it by then, it was too late to learn it. If I did know it, I couldn't know it any better. The most important thing for me at that time was to relax. I knew that my mind was trying to get me to check out this point or that point or to clarify something. The only way I could conquer this battle with myself was to throw myself into an activity totally unrelated to my courses. I worked on my jumpshot or forehand instead of the law. At night I further relaxed with James Bond or Marilyn Monroe.

As a result, when I went into my exams, my mind was completely relaxed and the secret mechanism worked perfectly. I was confident that when I read the exam, my mind would perform and I let it.

It's the same with an interview. If you have done adequate preparation stop, relax, and just let it work. You will react in accordance with your ability and preparation. As a result you will be yourself rather than something your mind is telling you you should be.

Maxwell Maltz has some things to say about relaxation that are to the point:

> Conscious effort inhibits and "jams" the automatic creative mechanism. The reason some people are self-conscious and awkward in social situations is simply that they are too consciously concerned, too anxious, to do the right thing. They are painfully conscious of every move they make. Every action is "thought-out." Every word spoken is calculated for its effect. We speak of such persons as "inhibited," and rightly so. But it would be more true were we to say that the "person" is not inhibited; but that the person has "inhibited" his own creative mechanism. If these people could "let go," stop trying, not care, and give no thought to the matter of their behavior, they could act creatively, spontaneously, and "be themselves."

CHECKLIST

★ Continue to tell yourself that you are doing well.

★ Even if you don't believe in yourself, try to make the interviewer think that you do.

★ Keep your doubts to yourself.

★ An interview is centered on the subject you know best— yourself.

★ Don't let rejection erode your confidence.

★ The interviewer knows less about you than you do.

★ If you've done your preparation, you know more about her and her company than she knows about you.

★ Don't let the advice of others shake your confidence in yourself.

★ Interviewers expect a certain amount of nervousness.

★ Try to avoid sweaty palms by sitting with your palms exposed to air.

★ Combat nervousness by relaxing your muscles and getting enough sleep.

★ Remember—before the interview you don't have an offer. The worst that can happen is that after the interview you still won't have an offer.

★ If you see something you want, go after it.

★ Don't worry about failure.

★ Don't look back.

★ Don't make tension-causing judgments.

★ Go into the interview with one of your objectives being that you are also interviewing the company to find out about it.

★ Trust yourself to react properly.

★ In order to relax mentally, you must first relax your body.

★ Stop preparing the night before the interview at the latest.

DRESS

The initial impression you make on the interviewer (and, in this chapter, let's assume the interviewer's a man) creates a presumption in his mind that will have a strong effect on the rest of the interview. He will look at you and form an opinion about you based on your appearance. How you are dressed will make up 80 percent of this opinion, and it will be formed before you open your mouth.

A television commercial claimed that "image is everything." Despite the hyperbole of this claim, the way in which you dress will certainly have an effect on the interviewer's initial impression of you. If there is something bizarre or slovenly about your dress, it may be a deciding factor in the result of the interview.

You should dress with consideration for three factors: 1. Dress to your advantage; 2. Dress to suit your interviewer; and, 3. Dress appropriately for the position for which you are interviewing.

Dress to your advantage

Dressing to your advantage means that you should dress in a manner that puts you in the most favorable light and does not offend. Your attire can speak for you as strongly as what you say. Your choice of colors should blend well. If they do not, this will be a point that could stand out in your interviewer's mind to your detriment. Do you want to be remembered as "that person, wearing purple and pink"? A garish combination of colors will probably make more of an impression than any profound argument you make. How would you react if you were an interviewer and someone walked in wearing a red-checked sports jacket, a purple striped shirt, and a pink polka-dot tie? Your lasting impression would probably be of the horrendous outfit he chose to wear and your confidence in his judgment would be permanently impaired. If you lack confidence in your judgment, seek the advice of someone qualified, like a friend whose style of dress you admire, a wardrobe consultant, or a department store sales clerk who exhibits good taste.

Dress conservatively

For most positions, the safest bet is to dress conservatively. It is risky to wear trendy styles. Although even corporation presidents now sport longer hair, when the Beatles first wore their hair long, those who copied them were viewed as freaks. **It takes a long period of time for a fad to become a style. Wait until it's accepted before you adopt it for an interview.**

Dress for the interviewer

Remember the story I referred to earlier of the law school student who came to an interview with me dressed in an old sweatshirt with holes in it, dirty blue jeans, and scuffed sneakers. **Don't try to make some childish point of being antiestablishment or independent by dressing in a manner that will offend your interviewer.** If you care enough to go to the interview, why blow it by dressing in a manner that tells the interviewer, "I don't give a damn about you"?

Don't dress in a manner that will cause your interviewer to draw an unfavorable impression from your dress prior to starting the interview. If you stick to conservative dress you're going to be safe.

Jocelyn Young, national accounts manager for Datapro, a division of McGraw Hill, offers a few tips:

> For mid- to high-level positions, you can expect to go through at least four interviews in one day. My main advice may sound trivial, but it's actually very practical: Don't wear anything that wrinkles easily! You need to look "together" for a full day. Don't try to dress to please any one audience, either. You will probably be interviewed by co-workers as well as those who would be in positions above and below you. Your best bet is to find out what the standard of dress is where you are interviewing, and not deviate from it too much.

Jolly Mansfield-Young, area systems manager for Tandem Computers, says that all prospective employees at their Dallas headquarters, from the lowest to the highest positions, undergo two preliminary screening interviews. Those who pass the screening process are invited back for a second round of interviews. They can expect to be interviewed by at least five employees of the company all on one day, and their interviewers will come from all levels of the organization. Mansfield-Young does a fair amount of interviewing herself, and in terms of dress, this is what she has to say:

> Don't wear clothes that will detract from you as a person. You don't want the interviewer to focus on your clothes rather than your abilities. On the other hand, avoid an overly packaged "dress-for-success" look. This always sets off an alarm for me and causes me to probe a little more deeply than I ordinarily would because I feel I need to find the person under the wrappings. Whatever

you decide to wear, make sure that it feels comfortable to you. The interview day is going to be long and stressful, and you don't want to be fidgeting with buttons or tight cuffs or shoes you've never worn before. You always want to give the interviewer the impression that you are completely at ease and in control, but if you're fussing with your clothes or have a pinched look, you'll destroy that illusion right away.

Color

There is a great deal of disagreement as to whether color has any effect upon a person with whom you come into contact. If you dress for an interview as if you are going to a funeral, you'll be at a disadvantage with one who dresses like springtime unless Dracula is your interviewer.

For what it's worth, the book *Color in Your World* treats the effect of colors upon the human psyche:

- If you like red, you are optimistic, restless, and passionate.
- If you like pink (and admit it), you are probably a woman. Among women, pink relates to "wealth, social advantage and to a sheltered, indulgent existence."
- If you like orange, you are good-natured but fickle, unsteady, and vacillating.
- If you like yellow, you are high-minded, introspective and contemplative, aloof, and given more to theory than action.
- If you like green you are affectionate, loyal, frank, and civic minded.
- If you like blue, you are deliberate and introspective, sensitive, and conservative.
- If you like brown, you are conscientious, shrewd, and obstinate.
- If you like grey, you are cautious and a compromiser.
- If you like black, you are sophisticated and dignified.

Obviously you are not going to be judged by an interviewer on a strict a scale as this, but you should know that there can be subconscious reactions to the colors you use in your dress. So don't use this chart as a basis for dressing for interviews, but consider that some people do make judgments based upon appearance. Movies have educated us to expect certain professions when we see specific types of dress. A trench coat means a private detective. White tie on a dark shirt means a gambler. Black leather jacket over a white tee shirt means a motorcycle tough.

I remember attending a meeting with a client who was looking for millions of dollars in financing. He had been told that the person with whom we were meeting had access to Middle-Eastern money. We set up a meeting with him at a restaurant in Los Angeles, but when he showed up, I immediately sensed that we were wasting our time. He was dressed in a loud sports coat and a cravat. He hadn't uttered a word, but my reaction to him was that he was a flaky promoter.

Unfortunately, my initial impression proved to be accurate. We were forced to sit and listen to his pitch for more than two hours, two hours of name dropping and grandiose schemes to finance my client's enterprise. I didn't say anything after he departed but asked my client what he thought. His reaction was instantaneous: "Two hours of nothing," he said.

Scents

Other questions arise regarding grooming. If you're a woman how much perfume, if any, should you wear? If you're a man, should you wear an after-shave? Scents are important. Remember that the interviewer is going through many interviews, and he may work in the room in which he interviews you. So you want to be sure that your scent doesn't linger after you.

If you wear perfume or after-shave or some other kind of lotion that emits an odor, there are two cardinal rules. First, make sure that none of it is on your hands so that it is not transferred to the interviewer when you shake hands. Second, be sure that it is not so strong that it will waft through his room the rest of the day. You don't want him to remember you because of a lingering smell, no matter how expensive the aroma.

Dress for the job

There is another thing to consider when it comes to your mode of dress. What kind of job are you interviewing for? Although generally an interviewee should avoid extremes, this is not always true. For example, if a woman is interviewing for a job as a cocktail waitress, part of the qualification for the position might be sex appeal, so dressing for the interview in a way that highlights your sensuality could be a plus for several reasons. First, it would relieve the interviewer of having to ask whether or not you would be willing to dress in a sexually provocative way. This is a question that could cause the interviewer to worry about your filing a claim for sexual discrimination, especially if the interviewer is a man. If you relieve him from the burden of asking it by the way you dress, it could be a big relief. Second, it would show the interviewer how you looked without the interviewer having to guess or ask you to put on the costume he might want you to wear. Third, it indicates in a nonverbal way that you know what's involved in the job and that you are experienced.

On the other hand, if you were to dress for an interview for a position in industry in a sexually provocative way, it could leave a distinctly negative impression since sex appeal would have no earthly relationship to such a job. It could communicate the wrong impression or, worse, be seen as an invitation, or the interviewer could draw the conclusion that you feel you aren't qualified for the position but are trying to get the job just on the basis of sex appeal.

But no matter what kind of job you're interviewing for, you should dress neatly. Even if you're interviewing to be a laborer or ditch digger, dressing in a clean and neat manner will indicate that you have enough interest in the job to take the time to dress well. It's never a plus to show up in dirty, unkempt clothes, no matter what the job.

Women in management

As women move up the ladder in management, problems relating to sex are evolving, but it's still the fact that there are far more men than women in upper management. Women who are interviewing for positions in management have unique problems. One Los Angeles attorney who has worked for a major Wall Street law firm and a major New York Stock Exchange corporation says:

> I'm a fanatic on how women should dress for an interview. I never wear pants and I always wear very conservative dresses, on the long side, never anything short, never anything low cut, never anything too flamboyant. Most of my things are solid colors. I dress in pastels or navy and black and brown. It's hard to tell me from a secretary anyway. If I go in dressed too much like a secretary, I get taken for a secretary. It also makes me look more professional. I want to look good in what I buy. I certainly don't tie my hair back and wear horned-rim glasses and no makeup. But I think it looks more professional and businesslike and gains me better acceptance to dress conservatively."

She varies this theme, however, when interviewing with someone nearer her own age. "When I know I'm going to be interviewing a man who is close to my own age, I try to wear something softer, like a baby blue or a light green, maybe even a pink because it makes me seem less threatening to him. It looks more feminine. It looks softer. It looks less professional and therefore he feels less challenged by me."

She has had several interviewing experiences where the combination of her sex and aggressiveness cost her offers. One firm made her an offer and then withdrew it; the younger members in the firm argued that she threatened to wreck the close, noncompetitive atmosphere they had created in the firm. She combats this feeling by looking more feminine and therefore less aggressive when she interviews younger men. She puts a large emphasis on colors. Her experience has proven to her that the way she dresses has a very important effect on the interview.

Cleanliness

There is one constant that applies to both men and women. No matter what your sex and no matter what type of job you are interviewing for, be neat and clean.

- **Be sure that your fingernails are properly cut and clean.** Dirty fingernails can result in a feeling of revulsion in an interviewer that you will be unable to counter.

- **Ensure that your hair is neat.** If you have to park outside the building where you are having the interview, the wind may mess up your hair. Try to visit a restroom and inspect your coiffure before going into your interview.

- **Your clothes should be neat and pressed, and your shoes should not be scuffed.** Jeri Long, a Bank of America executive, says, "Scuffed, dirty, and poorly maintained shoes account for the highest rejection percentage of all clothing atrocities."

- **Be careful about the amount of jewelry you wear.** An armful of bracelets and a handful of rings can leave a negative impression.

- **If you are bothered by bad breath, take a breath mint before entering the interview.** If your interview is in the afternoon, don't have a cocktail at lunch. The smell of liquor on the breath will not be received favorably. Also be careful of what you eat before your interview. If you eat Italian food, for example, you may come across as one huge garlic clove to your interviewer.

- **Be sure you bathe before the interview.** There is probably no bigger turnoff for an interviewer than to interview someone who has body odor. If you've got this problem more severely than others, try to bathe just before leaving for the interview and use a deodorant-antiperspirant.

- **Your clothes should be fresh.** If you have a suit, shirt, or dress that you've worn once and feel that you can get another wearing out of it before sending it to the cleaners, get the additional wearing some other time. If you wear freshly cleaned and pressed clothes, you won't have to worry about your clothes being spotty, wrinkled, or smelly. Robert H. Lentz, former vice-president and chief counsel for Litton Industries, sums it up well: "Personal appearance and personal habits are very important. If an interviewee has bad breath or body odor I'd say that it implies a certain sloppiness that's personal. I think that there's an inference of some value that if a person is sloppy in appearance or has a greasy tie, for example, or a very cavalier outfit going out for a job interview, it implies that the person is possibly sloppy in many ways. I would consider that a very definite negative. I think that personal appearance is highly important. **Even though it's a first impression, people have to realize that when they're being interviewed they're trying to convey as much as possible to the interviewer in a very limited amount of time. Proper dress and good personal appearance are both important."**

CHECKLIST

★ Dress to your advantage.

★ Dress to suit your interviewer.

★ Dress for the position for which you are interviewing.

★ Your colors and patterns should coordinate.

★ Dress conservatively.

★ Consider the effect your choice of colors will have.

★ Do not dress sensually unless sex appeal is part of the job.

★ Your fingernails should be clean and properly cut.

★ Your hair should be neat and combed.

★ Check out your appearance in a mirror before entering the interview.

★ Your clothes should be fresh, neat, and pressed.

★ Your shoes should not be scuffed.

★ Your jewelry should be sparse.

★ If you have bad breath, take a breath mint.

★ Don't drink liquor before an interview.

★ Don't eat foods that will leave an odor on your breath before an interview.

★ Bathe and use a deodorant-antiperspirant before the interview.

SILENCE AND POWER

In the late nineteenth century, Adrian (Cap) Anson was the premier baseball player in the National League. He batted more than .400 and fielded flawlessly. But one thing bugged Anson, and in 1888 he did something about it.

Anson organized a group of fellow baseball players and demanded that African Americans be prohibited from playing in the National League. Because of his prestige and the tenor of the times, an unwritten law was maintained, and thereafter not an African American player's name graced the box scores of the major leagues, despite such standout players as Josh Gibson, Satchel Paige, and James (Cool Papa) Bell.

In 1945, a grizzled baseball executive had a plan. Branch Rickey was general manager of the Brooklyn Dodgers, and he told his scout, Clyde Sukeforth, to go to Chicago, check out a player's arm and, if satisfied that his arm was sound, bring him to Brooklyn for an interview.

Sukeforth returned a few days later, and he and Jackie Robinson entered Rickey's office. Sukeforth told Rickey that he hadn't seen Robinson's arm but had brought him in for Rickey to interview anyway.

After introductions, Rickey subjected Robinson to intense study. No one said a word as Rickey stared at Robinson for several minutes. Finally Rickey told Robinson that for years he had been looking for a great black baseball player, that he had a feeling that Robinson was his man. But he said that he needed someone who was more than a great athlete; he needed someone who could take insults and abuse and have the courage not to fight back. He described the terrible abuse that Robinson would have to take from everyone—fellow players, fans, sports writers, even his own teammates. But Rickey said if the first black man to play baseball in the National League in fifty years fought back, he'd set the cause back twenty years.

When Rickey was through, he waited for Robinson's response. But Robinson didn't say anything. For five minutes the room was enmeshed in silence as Robinson thought and Rickey waited. Sukeforth said that Rickey was immensely impressed that Robinson did not give a quick answer.

Finally Robinson told Rickey that he had no doubts about his ability to play baseball in the National League but that that judgment would be up to Rickey. He promised that if Rickey were willing to take the risk there would not be any incident. Thus ended a classic interview, one that changed not only the complexion of the sporting world but the opportunities of African Americans in all professions.

Jackie Robinson was a man of power, as was Branch Rickey. Their initial meeting emphasizes the manifestation of power through silence. Each used silence, but in a different way and with different purposes.

Silence by the interviewer

When they first met, Rickey said nothing, staring at Robinson for several minutes. Rickey was applying stress before he uttered a word. Robinson responded by withstanding the scrutiny with silence and confidence. It was Rickey's move. Had Robinson fidgeted or shown discomfiture, Rickey's impression would probably have been less favorable. Rickey had been looking for forty years to break the color line. A few more years wouldn't matter. He had to have the man who could stand the tension under which he would be put. He had to have a man of power and restraint.

The thinking silence

After Rickey had put the facts before Robinson, Robinson was silent. He had the confidence in himself to think the problem through, and he wasn't intimidated by the powerful man across the desk from him. The room was filled with silence for five minutes. Someone who is uncomfortable with himself, or is intimidated, or lacks confidence, will find five minutes of silence in the same room with a man of power and decision an eternity. But Robinson thought the problem through. He didn't rush out with a rapid acceptance, which could have been his undoing. **He thus showed Rickey that he had the confidence in himself to consider the proposition as something that could expose him to great risk and that he wasn't going to jump at an opportunity without considering the consequences.**

Each of these men conveyed his power to the other through silence. Although Rickey used silence as a tool, Robinson was not trained in interviewing and was reacting from within. His silence was a genuine indication of the man inside.

Most people tend to think it is their obligation to fill gaps in conversation. They feel an urge to talk when there is silence. But sometimes silence on the part of an interviewer invites initiative by the interviewee. Other times it does not. It's important to recognize one from the other.

Silence you should not break

In the Robinson-Rickey interview, it was clear that Rickey's initial silence did not invite conversation from Robinson. It's very rare that in an employment interview a candidate will be met with such a stressful imposition of silence upon introduction.

If you are alert, you may be able to distinguish an invitation from an evaluation. In *Contact: The First Four Minutes,* authors Leonard and Natalie Zunin say, "Once people are talking, they look at their partners less often than when they listen. To look away while speaking is natural. . . . A pause while glancing away usually means an incomplete phrase, signaling, 'I have not yet said all I want to say; don't interrupt.'"

Silence as a plea for help

Often silence does invite initiative. I remember an interview I had with a potential client. The president of the company was fairly shy. I accompanied the vice president to the president's office and the interview consisted mostly of my talking with the vice president while the president observed.

Nobody asked me questions. We were introduced, and the three of us just sat there looking at one another. It was clearly an invitation for me to take over the interview, so I started discussing a real estate project I was working on, which I had discussed previously with the vice president. We chatted about this, and then I slowly introduced other areas in which I had worked that I felt were germane to the operations of the company.

The president hardly uttered a word. After I felt that I had established my credentials, I asked the president to tell me something about his company and its problems and why he felt that he needed a lawyer.

The dichotomy between the initial silence in this situation and the Robinson-Rickey silence was determined by the ambience of the confrontations. There was nothing friendly about the Rickey silence. It was plainly evaluative. On the other hand the silence that greeted me in the president's office was expectant. Had Robinson started to talk while Rickey was staring at him, or had I remained silent while the president waited, we each would have misjudged the situation and most probably blown the interview.

How to endure stressful silence

Silence is a powerful phenomenon that can produce intriguing effects. Using it as an interview technique is simple. Sometime around the middle of the interview, the interviewer (and, for this chapter, let's assume the interviewer is a woman) will ask a question requiring a short answer. She gets the short answer. Then she does not respond. Nothing. She just sits there, looking at you but saying nothing.

The predictable result is that the silence will cause you to think about your frailties. You will begin to worry that you have said the wrong thing, or that your nose is running, your clothing is unbuttoned, or your hair is out of place. So without thinking, you rush to correct whatever it is that is worrying you. You restate something you said earlier, wipe your nose, brush the hair back. All of these actions are telltale signs of insecurity in the face of silence.

Since the cause of the insecurity is derived from an active mind, the cure is to keep your mind busy with other matters. You know that the best way to handle silence is simply to return the interviewer's stare with a calm, anticipatory look. If your mind is racing trying to determine which weakness she's focusing on, you're going to fidget by going directly to your supposed weakness. The solution is to keep your mind too busy to think about your weaknesses.

The best way I have discovered to do this is to become aware of the silence and see how long it lasts. The moment that you recognize that the interviewer is imposing silence, start counting to yourself to see how long it lasts. I'll guarantee that it won't be longer than fifteen seconds. Start counting to yourself "one thousand-one, one thousand-two" and so on until she breaks the silence. You'll be so busy ensuring that your one-thousands actually equal one second that your mind won't focus on your runny nose or falling hair. Your demeanor will reflect a calm anticipation, and suddenly your test will be over and the interviewer will continue the interview by breaking the silence with another question.

Don't retract

The most common reaction to the deliberately introduced stressful silence is to conclude that you've somehow stuck your foot in your mouth. You hastily review the answer you just gave and your instinct is to retract or qualify it. DON'T! Don't retract! Don't change what you've said, even if you think the interviewer doesn't agree with you or is looking for a different answer.

A small digression here may emphasize this point. It is said that in the first year of law school, the professors try to scare you to death. Law school is generally taught by the Socratic, or question-and-answer, method where the professor quizzes a student about a case the class has read. The professor will get the student to take a stand and then caustically tear the position to shreds.

Contracts professor Richard Speidel was feared at Virginia Law School for his brutality to the students' psyches. It was the rule rather than the exception that he would keep a student standing for the entire hour grilling him on points of contract law. Sometimes he would start the next class with the person who had been destroyed the previous session, so you could never relax.

But there was a rule to Speidel's game, and it is a cardinal rule that is also applicable to interviewing: If you stuck to your guns and didn't change your position when he attacked you, he'd let you sit down after about fifteen minutes.

One day he called on me and had me brief a case about a crew of a merchant ship who agreed to ship out for a certain rate; when the ship hit the high seas, the crew struck for three times the rate previously agreed upon.

"Well, Mr. Medley," said Mr. Speidel, "what would you do if the ship's owner called you for advice?"

"I'd tell him to go ahead and agree to pay the rate and then renege when the cargo was unloaded at destination," I replied.

"What!" exploded Speidel. "You'd have the ship's owner make a commitment he never had any intention of honoring?"

"Well," I countered, "I'd say that he was acting under undue duress and that he wasn't bound because the crew's actions were a breach of contract."

"Do you mean, Mr. Medley, that he honor only the commitments he wants to honor, those that work to his advantage, and ignore those that work to his disadvantage? What is this, Mr. Medley," he attacked with devastating vitriol, "the two-edged sword of Damocles?"

He leaned against the blackboard and waited. Well, I thought, he's certainly got a good point. Maybe I should reconsider. Maybe he'll like me better if I agree with him and will treat me more easily. But then I remembered how he had changed and destroyed people before. If I change, he'll keep switching and I'll never sit down. Taking a deep breath, I gambled on a little show of strength and confidence in my position. "Not for my client," I replied. "He would be sticking by the original agreement."

He glared for a minute and then, with a smirk, said, "You may sit down, Mr. Medley." My ordeal for the year was over; it had lasted less than ten minutes.

When silence is used as a method of challenging your belief in your statements, you can be devastated. If you are faced with this situation and if you've taken a position, don't backtrack. Just sit and wait. Generally in an interview it's not what you say when you voice your opinions; it's whether you have the confidence in them.

Silence and Power

Don't mutter

A second mistake that is made in the face of silence is to start to mutter. You may have given an opinion and the interviewer just sits there looking at you. So you add something on to it. She still says nothing, so you add something else.

If you've said what you have to say on a subject, stop. If she doesn't immediately pick up the conversation, you have no obligation to continue talking. Muttering and frivolous talking in the face of silence indicate a lack of confidence and the fact that the tension she has created is getting to you. So don't add taglines to your opinions. If you're through talking on a subject, let it be.

Just wait calmly

Silence is easy to handle if you recognize it quickly for what it is: a ploy. The interviewer is testing you. The best way to survive it is to sit calmly and wait for her to continue the interview. Don't fidget. Don't look down or around. Just sit and look at her expectantly. The silence cannot last long because the interview is for a short period of time, and there are many things she wants to cover. If you're not ready for the silence, it may seem to last an eternity. If you are prepared and recognize it, it will be over in a few seconds and you may have conveyed more than you could have with thousands of words.

A sophisticated interviewer will introduce stressful silence at a time when you least expect it. If you are prepared for it and handle it properly, you will get one of the warmest, positive feelings you'll ever receive out of an interview. If you remember what has been said here and if you're relaxed and confident, you should be able to handle stressful silence whenever it's introduced.

Breaking the stressful silence

There are two good ways for an interviewee to handle silence introduced into an interview as an imposition of stress.

The first is to sit expectantly, as I explained earlier. The second involves a risk and must be handled adroitly. You have finished your answer to one of the questions and the interviewer just sits and stares, and you recognize that stress has been introduced. **Who should break the silence?** As we have seen, changing your statement or backtracking or muttering can be interpreted as a lack of confidence in yourself and what you have said. If a few seconds pass and you know the interviewer is using silence as stress and not just thinking over your answer or preparing a new question, you may ask, "Do you mind if I ask a few questions about your company [or the job or yourself]?" This breaks the silence in an acceptable manner without revealing an insecurity on your part or any inability to handle the silence. It also takes the silence away from her as a weapon.

By asking a question pertinent to the interview, you are telling the interviewer that you recognize that the interview is for a finite period of time and you want to cover as many areas as possible. There is quite a bit of information you wish to obtain from her, and this seems like a good spot in the interview to get it. You tacitly don't recognize her imposition of stress for what it is. Instead you are telling her, "Well, if you're through, there are some things I'd like to ask."

Just remember: if you break the silence, don't do it by volunteering more information, either on the subject just finished or on a different subject. If you do, you will indicate a lack of ability to deal with the silence, and this can be a big negative. If you have communicated by your method of speaking that you have finished talking on the subject under discussion (which is generally done by pausing and looking at the interviewer), you must keep it closed. By bringing the subject up again in response to the silence, you will probably have failed the silence test. Similarly, by bringing up an entirely new subject after you have signaled that you have finished speaking, you express your insecurity. After you have indicated that you've finished speaking, don't begin again unless it's to ask some questions.

Silence by the interviewee

It is possible for you, the interviewee, to introduce silence into the interview for your own benefit. In Chapter 5, I suggested that pausing for a minute or so not only gives you time to think over your answer, it also indicates to the interviewer that you are a deliberate person, not given to making snap decisions. Eisenhower, you remember, requested several hours to contemplate. Robinson took five minutes to think over and formulate his answer. Each man used silence as a tool to indicate self-confidence and restraint. Most important of all, each conveyed his power through the use of silence.

The way you answer a difficult question may convey more than the answer itself. If you give a quick answer, for example, you may leave a bad impression. An answer given too quickly, without sufficient thought, may lead the interviewer to think you are a person of little depth.

Perhaps the most important aspect of Rickey's evaluation was the fact that Robinson sat silent for five minutes before answering. Remember, Rickey had not offered him a job. He had merely said, "I have reason to believe that you're [my] man." Unquestionably the manner of Robinson's response was what decided the day. Had Robinson said without a pause that he wanted the job, Rickey undoubtedly would have concluded that Robinson either did not recognize the turmoil into which he would be entering or was insincere in his promise to avoid incidents.

But Robinson thought through what he had just heard. By his silence, he conveyed to Rickey the fact that he recognized the risks and the tremendous self-control that would be required of him.

Look at it from Rickey's viewpoint. African American ballplayers had been yearning for more than fifty years to get into organized baseball. He was making an offer that thousands of African American men had dreamed of for a half-century. Rickey knew that Robinson was no different from any other African American ballplayer. He wanted to play in organized baseball, where the money and fame were. But Rickey had to be convinced that Robinson recognized the risks involved and what would be required of him.

The fact that Robinson did not jump for the plum but thought about it for a long period before replying convinced Rickey probably even before he heard the answer that Robinson was his man. It was the silence, not the words, that did it.

Successfully handling silence in an interview is a most convincing demonstration of power and self-confidence. If you get into a silence situation and use it properly, you can't help but win. If the interviewer knows what she's doing, and you know what you're doing, your feeling of having handled the situation properly will be instantaneous.

Some interviewers are actually more nervous than the people they are interviewing, in which case a long silence may mean they can't think of anything to say and that they'd be grateful if you would help them through these awkward pauses. You must learn to recognize whether you are talking to a sophisticated interviewer or to an inexperienced one so that you can distinguish a stressful silence from a plea for help to keep the conversation flowing.

One of the keys to look for in making this determination is whether the interviewer looks at you. If she does and says nothing, she is obviously introducing stress, and you should act accordingly. If, on the other hand, she looks away, fidgets, or exhibits other nervous mannerisms, she probably can't think of anything to say and is wondering how she's ever going to get through this interview.

Don't delude yourself by thinking that this situation never happens. Many selection interviewers are inexperienced, and more than you might imagine are terrified of interviews. They are on uncertain ground, and a lot of them are just as worried that they are going to make fools of themselves in front of you as you are that you're going to make a fool of yourself in front of them.

In such a situation, you should come to the interviewer's rescue by telling her you have some questions. She will undoubtedly ask to hear them, and you can then inquire about the job, the company, or the interviewer herself. She should feel relief and indebtedness to you for saving her from embarrassment and for not exposing her inexperience.

CHECKLIST

★ Silence by the interviewer is generally an imposition of stress.

★ Silence by the interviewee is a manifestation of confidence.

★ Don't break a stressful silence imposed by the interviewer except to ask a question.

★ The interviewer will cue you as to when she wants you to break the silence.

★ If the silence is not imposed as stress, it's your obligation to break it.

★ Don't retract in the face of silence.

★ Don't mutter in the face of silence.

★ Wait through a stressful silence by counting the seconds it lasts.

★ Don't fidget through a stressful silence.

★ If you recognize that the interviewer is inexperienced and her silence is a plea for help, break it by asking questions.

SEX

One of the most controversial aspects of interviewing for a job involves sex. Since the original publication of *Sweaty Palms* in 1978, there has been a revolution in the treatment of sex. In 1978, sex in the job market was still treated with a wink and a nod. *Sweaty Palms* was one of the first to raise the issue and deal with it head on.

There are three basic ways that sex may become an issue in a job interview. The first is alleged sexual harassment by the interviewer. The second is the use of sexual attractiveness by the interviewee to get a job. The third is the pursuit of a sexual relationship by the interviewer, which is part of sexual harassment, but will be dealt with separately in this chapter so that you are aware of it and are prepared for it.

153

Sexual harassment

Sexual harassment in the workplace has been clearly defined and outlawed by both state and federal law. As an example, California law now defines sexual harassment as unwanted sexual advances, or visual, verbal, or physical conduct of a sexual nature. The California Department of Fair Employment and Housing has compiled a list of offensive behavior that includes unwanted sexual advances, leering, making sexual gestures, making or using derogatory comments and jokes, verbal sexual advances or propositions, and touching.

Both federal and state law recognize two types of sexual harassment: *quid pro quo*, or the grant or denial of employment based on sexual favors, and *hostile work environment*, or the deprivation of the right to work in an environment free from discriminatory intimidation, ridicule, and insult. Even someone not personally subjected to the harassment may make a claim if forced to work in an atmosphere where harassment exists.

Today any relatively sophisticated interviewer should be aware of the risks involved in including any kind of sexual elements in an interview. But the fact is that many interviewers are unaware of what may and what may not be done in an interview. It's not improbable that an interviewee will be faced with a sexual harassment issue in an interview without the interviewer even knowing that the issue has been introduced. It's also possible that an interviewer will *intentionally* violate the rules against sexual harassment. The question is, if you're presented with the problem, whether innocently or intentionally (and that distinction may not be something that you will find easy to determine), how should you handle it?

Before I go on I want to emphasize that this applies equally to both men and women interviewees. However, because of the preponderance of men in upper management, most sexual harassment occurs with women as the victims. As more and more women become involved in management, this is changing, but the fact is that, at present, women are still far and away more often victim than victimizer.

In a job interview, sexual harassment most commonly occurs in the form of an offensive question. When you are asked a question that offends you, the first thing you must determine is whether there is a business reason for asking the question. If you think there is none (like asking you if you are sleeping with anybody), then you should handle it in the manner discussed in Chapter 5, "The Question and the Answer."

The problem with the offensive question is that more often than not it is not intended to be offensive. The perfect example of this is a question that is asked primarily of women, "Have you completed your family?" or its corollary: "Do you plan on having any (more) children?" (The legality of this question is covered later in the chapter on discrimination. The problem is that, legal or not, it is often asked, and you must be prepared to handle it properly.) Many women immediately react by thinking, "They don't ask men this question, so why are they asking me? It's discriminatory and demeaning." Undoubtedly true, but you must realize that there may be a business reason (maybe it's not legitimate, but it **is** a business reason) for asking. Put yourself in the place of an employer. You are interviewing to fill a vacancy that happens to be a key position. You have budgeted that this position will be filled by a person who will assume a large responsibility load; that person is needed every day. You have also budgeted that the person filling this position will be absent from the job for two weeks each year for vacation and probably an additional five days because of illness. So you are counting on the person to be on the job forty-nine weeks each year.

If you're interviewing a young married woman who has a two-year-old child, for example, you may think, "Well, she's young and married and already has a child. If she gets pregnant, she'll probably have to miss several weeks while having her child. That's on top of her vacation and normal illnesses. Who's going to fill in for her while she's off? Do I have to train someone just to be her stand-in while she has children?"

If you as interviewee recognize this worry, you may not be able to answer the interviewer adequately, but you won't make the mistake of reacting with hostility—and that's the worst thing that you can do. Try to recognize that the question is not necessarily being asked to put you down or to discriminate against you but to voice a concern.

A reader from Shawnigan Lake, British Columbia, Canada, writes about how she was subjected to what she considered to be sexual harassment and how she felt and reacted:

> I was already employed as a secretary but when the manager's job for a local tourist association came open I decided I would try for it. (I have a bachelor's degree in mass communications and have experience as a newspaper editor and reporter). I sent in my resume and got a copy of the association's yearly publication to learn the names of the board and whatever I could about the association's goals and past successes. I went so far as to plan some ideas that could be used to help publicize the region (one of their main goals). After doing all that I felt confident that I could at least present myself as an intelligent person who could do the job.
>
> I was interviewed by a panel of three; each person in turn asked me a series of questions they had written down on a piece of paper. I felt I answered the questions well and was able to present my ideas, which they all seemed interested in and even enthusiastic about. Then it happened!
>
> One of the interviewers started asking questions that I didn't want to answer like "Your résumé doesn't say but are you married?". I answered this question but thought it had no relevance to the job. The next question was "Does your husband have a good job?" I asked him to clarify what he meant. "Is he going to be transferred out of the area soon?" I answered that he worked for a hospital and they didn't have a transfer policy that I knew of. Then he asked, "What are your family plans?" Right then I knew I should have said something like "I think what you're asking is if I will be committed to this job and the answer is yes," but I was so stunned by the question all I could answer was something about my husband and I not having decided what we were going to do since we hadn't been married that long. I finished the interview pleasantly but I was furious! How dare they ask those questions?
>
> Well, they offered the job to another candidate and I just continued on in my secretary's job. I did go back to one of the interviewers and asked why I didn't get the job. According to him it was because I couldn't work Friday nights and Saturdays due to my

religion. He also said I was an excellent candidate for the job and that if it ever came open again I should try for it. (Which to me didn't make sense because I wasn't going to change my religion for the job). At that point I told him that I regarded their questions about my personal life as not relevant to the job and in addition they were in direct violation of the Labor Rights Act. I gave him a brochure with a list of questions you can't ask during an interview or on a job application. . . .

Choosing the person with the best ability to do the job should be the only factor businesses take into consideration, not the sex of the individual. Young women can offer the best abilities to many companies but if they are not hired simply because they might get pregnant, then not only does the woman suffer but the company does and so does society. Instead it seems for men it's a competition to figure out who can do the best job; for women it's a competition to see who's least likely to get pregnant.

I guess what I'm trying so desperately to tell you is that I felt degraded that my abilities to do a job weren't as important as my private life. . . .

This woman's letter is typical of a lot of the mail I receive from people who didn't know how to answer a question that they considered offensive and have written to tell me of their problems and their real feelings. The solution? The expressions of her real feelings to me in her letter should have been how she answered the question!

You must realize that some of the questions interviewers ask are to resolve genuine concerns that they have. My advice here in *Sweaty Palms* is not to legitimize offensive or illegal questions; it is to explain the reasoning behind the questions so that an interviewee might be better prepared when hit with them. Maybe the interviewer's concerns are unfair; maybe their questions are illegal; but the concerns are there, and you are ahead of the game if they state them. The law can prohibit them from asking the question. The law can prohibit them from discriminating against you. But what the law cannot do is keep them from having the concerns, and the practical result of an unrectified concern can be your not being offered a job.

It's very easy for a prospective employer to refuse to hire a young woman on a pretext when the real concern is that she might get pregnant and want maternity leave, or that her husband might get a job and move somewhere else. If that occurs, it's up to you to prove that the reason was bogus and then go through litigation to try to win and recover damages. But is that the way you want to spend the next five years of your life?

Isn't it better to deal with the illegal question or the unexpressed fear openly and honestly? Had my reader expressed herself in her interview the way she expressed herself to me, she would have been much better off. Her eloquent expression of her feelings could only impress an interviewer. After all, the concern about her fecundity already existed. The way for her to combat it was to deal with it head on as she did in her letter to me.

Use of sex by the interviewee

Sex is a two-headed coin. Not only may an interviewer use sex as a form of harassment, a job-seeker may use it to try to get a job. This is a flip side that's rarely mentioned. I do not encourage people to go after a job using sex as a ploy, nor do I condone the practice. I am only recognizing the existence of this possibility and pointing out the pitfalls from both sides of such a tawdry encounter.

Most counselors will advise that sex in the office is a bad thing and that if you get a job because of it, everything will turn out poorly. Barbara Walters in her book, *How to Talk with Practically Anybody about Practically Anything,* says, "When to be sexy, and when not. When not is when applying for a job, or when trying to keep one. . . . The beddable look does not lead to the door marked President, but to the one marked Exit. Be sexy on your own time; working hours and job interviews require the crisp and cool version of you."

The Walters theory is based on the hypothesis that all interviewers are professional and are looking only for someone who can do the job. This may be true in a great many cases, but there are many interviewers who have a more hedonistic outlook on life. A top corporate executive told me a story that epitomizes the problem and its effects on all involved:

When I was a young manager, I had just joined a division and had to hire a secretary. I was sent one of the most beautiful, sensuous women I had ever seen. She was an absolute knockout. I interviewed her and while she played games with her eyes, I had enough self-control to determine that she couldn't type very well, wasn't very good at shorthand, didn't seem to be very well organized, and had very little experience in what I needed for a person to run my office. Reluctantly I told her that I didn't think she qualified for the job.

She was a friend of the person in charge of secretarial employment, so she got a job as a typist. Whenever an executive was looking for a secretary, she was the first one to be interviewed. Finally, after work one day, she met an executive who had one of the most efficient secretaries in the office. But this executive was the man for whom she was looking. He looked into her eyes and fired his secretary the next day.

She worked for him for several months, he became very morose because his work fell off, she received an offer to become secretary to the president of another company and left. She found a home as a window-dressing secretary to a company president who had others do the real work. The last I heard, everyone was happy except the guy who originally hired her. He never could find someone who managed his office the way his first secretary did.

It's true that there is a much-diminished chance that a job obtained on the basis of sexual attractiveness will last as long as one based upon ability. You should recognize the pitfalls if you are going to base your strategy on this. Walters thinks that office affairs inevitably lead to problems: "Most bosses are married men and so, unless it turns out to be for keeps and he goes the whole route of divorcing his wife and marrying you, the only way to end the affair will be to fire you."

If you get your job because of sex, once the sexual attraction ceases your performance will be subjected to the spotlight of attention. If you're not performing in your job and there is no more sexual attraction, you're probably going to be back in the job line pretty soon. If you enter on this path, you must change jobs pretty regularly.

The woman referred to above was wise; she made her move to a better job while she still had good credentials. Also her boss was beginning to cool on her and, given his

mental outlook, it was easier for him to give a good recommendation to get rid of her than to be truthful to the
prospective employer and then fire her.

If all you have to offer is sex, and you decide that this is
the route you're going to take, be sure you know the rules
of the game, but be prepared to ride the roller coaster.

Interviewer's sexual propositions

If you are attractive, articulate, and ambitious and are being
interviewed by a person of the opposite sex, there may come
a time when you feel you are being pursued for your sexual
attractiveness rather than your capabilities. It may not be
because of something overt; it will just be a feeling that you
have. What should you do? Should you bring it out in the
open? Should you react with indignation? Should you accept
an offer for a job if it is tendered?

Don't follow the first two alternatives. Your intuition may
be wrong, and to bring the question of sex out in the open
or react with indignation would result in an insult and almost certain withdrawal or lessening of interest. In this
situation, you must both analyze yourself and evaluate the
interviewer. If you have conducted a good interview yourself, you should have gained enough insight into the interviewer to make a judgment. Is the interviewer a professional
or one with hedonistic leanings?

If you're not sure whether the interest in you is because
you're capable or because of a sexual attraction, but you conclude that even though there are hedonistic leanings and
ulterior motives, the interviewer is still a professional and
will recognize and reward accomplishment, and if you're
confident you can do the job, you should leave your doubts
unspoken and pursue an offer. If your intuitions prove correct and there were ulterior motives, you can disabuse them
in a tactful way after you have the job. In the meantime, if
your performance has been good, you should have won a
respected place in the organization. You may never be sure
that the offer was not made because of sex, but what difference does it make? So long as you respect the interviewer's

professionalism and can handle the sexual advances when they come, you have achieved your objective—a job—and the fact that you may have gotten it because you're attractive is irrelevant. You should trade on what you have and use all your assets.

If, on the other hand, you do not gain a measure of respect and confidence in the interviewer's professionalism, you should trust your intuition and turn down the interest. A job that is taken on the basis of sex, when you want it on the basis of capability, can only lead to disaster if you don't want to participate in sexual games and your potential boss is not professional enough to recognize your talent in spite of your unwillingness to play. In this situation, trust your intuition and move on to interviews with others.

Caveat

We live in a litigious society. Many who feel that an interviewer is acting unprofessionally and pursuing an agenda more related to romance than to the job are quick to react with hostility, and immediately think about sexual harassment.

Dr. Benjamin Spock, in a passage that everyone in the job market should remember, said that people should have "sufficient sexual and romantic maturity to allow a person—man or woman—to show, whenever they are dealing with a member of the opposite sex, that they can be appropriately attentive and charming, without implying an intention of further seductiveness."

There is little that is more offensive than to have a well-intended compliment flung back in the face. If you think about it, your looks are just as important an asset as your brains or your grades or your experience. If you are a sensuous person, why downplay it?

The job market is a difficult field at best. In days of rising unemployment and expanding availability of workers, any asset you have should be used to your advantage. Sex must be used subtly, but it should not be ignored. If you've got it, don't flaunt it, but let it work naturally to your advantage.

CHECKLIST

★ Be aware of the rules relating to sexual harassment.

★ Try to determine whether your interviewer is applying sexual harassment *intentionally* or *innocently*.

★ If asked an offensive question, determine whether there is a business reason to ask it.

★ If asked an offensive question, answer with your honest feelings without being disagreeable.

★ Evaluate the interviewer's motivation.

★ Trust your intuition.

★ Recognize the pitfalls of accepting an offer based upon sex or the promise of sex.

★ If you accept a job based on sex appeal rather than skill, be prepared to change jobs often.

★ Don't react to genuine compliments with hostility.

★ If you feel a job is offered partly because of sexual attraction, but evaluate the interviewer as a professional and feel you can do a good job and be recognized for your work, don't turn the job down.

★ If you don't respect the interviewer as a professional, be wary of accepting an offer based partly on sexual attraction.

★ Don't be too sensitive.

SALARY

$\mathbf{P}$robably nothing worries an interviewee more than how to handle the subject of salary and benefits. For some reason, most job-hunters seem to feel that it is insulting to the employer to discuss salary. In fact, they often feel apologetic about it. On the other hand, a few job-seekers are very aggressive when it comes to salary negotiations, and look upon it as a challenge to push the stakes to the limit. There is no reason to feel apologetic, of course, but the subject of salary is something that you should handle very carefully.

Don't bring it up yourself

In the first place, this is one subject that you should not bring up yourself, at least not in the early stage of an interview when the interviewer (and, in this chapter, let's assume the interviewer is a man) is still sizing you up—trying to find out if you have the qualifications for the job and whether or not you are compatible. At this point, no interviewer, however inexperienced, wants to waste time discussing salary. So if you broach the subject yourself before he determines that he is interested in you, you run the very real risk of turning him off.

If there are several applicants interviewing for the same position, the interviewer has another reason for postponing discussion of salary. If he quotes a high salary to you, it makes it more difficult for him to negotiate salaries with the other applicants, who might have been happy with a lesser amount, or who might have been less qualified than you and therefore not worth the same high salary.

So leave the subject of salary for the interviewer to bring up. If, as the interview winds down, he asks you to come in for further interviews, or otherwise indicates that you are still being considered for the position, then you can risk bringing the subject up yourself. Simply ask what range of salary the position pays. Don't beat around the bush.

When you're asked how much you're making

One of the roughest problems faced by any interviewee comes when the interviewer asks how much the interviewee is making. Generally you are not making as much as you want to make or as much as you want your interviewer to offer you. As a general rule of thumb, someone who changes jobs wants an increase in salary of at least 20 percent. But what if you feel you are grossly underpaid and you want a much larger increase? What do you do when you are asked how much you are making?

It's a sad fact that employers will base their compensation more on what a candidate is making at his present job than on what the candidate is worth. If, for example, he has budgeted the job at $30,000 or $40,000 a year, and he finds that you are making $18,000 a year, it's unlikely that he'll offer you more than $22,000, even though he was originally willing to pay a lot more. Why? He knows he's in a buyer's market and your alternative is to stay where you are and continue making $18,000. He's not about to offer you a 50 percent increase when he can probably get you for a 20 percent increase.

So what do you do when he asks what you're making?

What you do **not** do is lie. You always run the risk of his verifying what you tell him. If you tell him you're making more than you actually are and he asks you for a W-2 or tax return or payroll stub, what can you say? If you refuse he'll assume that you were lying and will probably reject you on that basis alone.

An exception is that you can always refuse to supply a copy of your tax return when an interviewer requests it. Simply tell him that you never reveal such private and confidential information to anyone. He has no right to ask for such a legal document, and you have no obligation to supply it. The problem is that if he wants to verify what you've told him, he'll ask for some other type of verification, and you can't logically refuse a request he might make to have your present employer supply verification.

You do have one ploy you can try if he asks you for salary information before discussing what he is willing to pay for the position. Before replying, you can ask what the position pays. This turns the tables on him. If he asks for salary information, it's an indication that he is interested in you and that he is planning on discussing salary with you.

The problem with this query is that you risk being offensive. But if you are earning a very low salary in relation to what you want and what you think he's willing to pay, you've got to try something that will deflect him from his course of finding out your salary. It's possible that this query will permanently keep him off the subject, but it's not likely.

The advantage is that if he's broaching salary by asking how much you make, he's indicating that he's interested.

You must try and get him to reveal a salary range before you reveal how much you're making. If he tells you the range before you tell him that you make much less than that, it would be difficult and awkward for him to offer you less than the range he reveals. If you tell him your salary before he reveals the range, when he does indicate the range it'll be a lot lower than it was before you revealed your salary.

So the one rule to remember if you have a very low salary is to try to get him to tell you the salary range of the position for which you're interviewing **before** you tell him how much you're making.

When you're asked how much you want

If you are sure you know what you want and you express this in an interview, you must stick with it. Backing down will leave the impression that you are indecisive and lack integrity.

Several years ago, when a lawyer's pay was much lower than today, a young lawyer told me about his experience. He had interviewed with the general counsel for a fairly large corporation, and when the subject of salary came up he said that he would accept nothing less than $30,000. The interviewer said that this was beyond his budget, and tried to persuade him to accept $25,000. The candidate was firm. He wanted $30,000. Impressed, the interviewer recommended the candidate to the general counsel of another corporation who was also looking for an experienced attorney.

The interview with the second company went well, too, and when it came time to discuss salary, the young lawyer again said that he wanted $30,000. The interviewer, a dynamic individual, said that $26,000 was tops. The candidate hesitated. He was very interested in working for this second company, and the salary offer was closer to his goal. Besides, he had already priced himself out of one job, and was probably afraid it might happen again. So he asked for time to think about it.

The next day, the second interviewer called and told him that the offer was no longer open. Then the candidate called the first interviewer to see if the $25,000 offer was still good and was told that he was "too heavy" for the job. From having two corporations pursuing him, he was down to zero. What had happened? Simple. He had come across very strongly as a man who knew his worth and was willing to walk away from any offer less than $30,000. This was impressive and earned him the respect of both interviewers. But when he showed interest at the lower figure, it was a sign of equivocation that caused both interviewers to lose respect for him, resulting in rejection.

Had the young lawyer been more sophisticated or analyzed his position more carefully, he would have recognized the $26,000 offer as a blatant ploy. Since the first general counsel had recommended him to the second company, he could safely assume that the second counsel already knew that he wanted $30,000 and had turned down an offer of $25,000. He should have drawn the conclusion that the second company was willing to pay him what he wanted or they would not have wasted time interviewing him. The $26,000 offer was simply a part of their interview technique to test his character.

Once you present something as a requirement, you cannot back down, so don't paint yourself into a corner by trying a bluff you really don't believe in and are not willing to back all the way. Oscar-winning director Frank Capra tells of his first interview with the Mack Sennett, the "king of comedy" in the 1920s, and it is a good example of setting a requirement and sticking with it.

Capra had been writing "Our Gang" comedies for Hal Roach. But he wanted to be a director, so a friend arranged for an interview with Felix Adler, the head writer at Sennett's production company. After a short conversation with Adler, he was introduced to John Waldron, Sennett's accountant, who offered Capra $35 per week. Capra turned it down, saying that he got $40 at Roach.

Waldron wasn't impressed, saying that the rule was that beginners start at $35. Capra responded that he felt to take less than what he had been making would be going in the wrong direction and that he wanted to go toward the top. Waldron icily replied that when one works for Sennett, he's **at** the top and that $35 was his only offer. Capra could take it or leave it.

Capra said, "I swallowed hard [and said], 'Then I'll leave it, Mr. Waldron.' . . . My knees shook. I blew it. My big chance to work at Sennett's—and I blew it."

On the way out they stopped by Sennett's office. Waldron mentioned to Sennett that Capra wouldn't accept the beginner's $35 and that he wanted $45. Sennett asked Capra why he thought he was worth $45. Capra said, "Mr. Sennett, what's the difference what you pay me? If you don't think I'm worth it you'll fire me in two minutes anyway."

Sennett said that it was $35 or nothing, that he wouldn't break any of his own rules.

Capra replied, "Mr. Sennett, I'm not asking you to break **any** rules. John Waldron starts me on the books at $35. Okay? Tomorrow you raise me to $45. Everybody's happy and no rules broken."

Capra got the job. He knew what he wanted and was willing to walk away from the job rather than compromise. He stuck to his guns and got what he wanted.

Know yourself

In order to come out of the salary negotiation phase of your interview with self-respect, you need to plan and prepare by looking deeply into yourself and deciding the parameters of what you **must** have and what you would **like** to have. In discussing what you **must** have, you aren't losing anything by taking a firm stand.

In discussing points that you desire but can survive without always leave yourself an escape so that you can give in without losing face. Determining the difference between your needs and your desires is an essential part of your preparation, and it requires an honest analysis of yourself.

How much money you need

How much money you need and how much you desire are two completely different things.

You can determine how much you need by preparing a simple budget. How much does it cost you to live? Write down your rent or mortgage payment, how much you spend on food each month, what your car payments are, how much you spend on clothes, utilities, gasoline, cleaning, and so forth. Then check this with your monthly bank reconciliations for the past year. You may find that your memory is faulty and you're spending more than you realize. In any event, know exactly how much you have to earn in order to live. This is your basic salary requirement. You may **desire** more money (don't we all?), but you can live on this amount. So if worse comes to worse and an offer is made for a job you would enjoy and it meets this amount, you can take it without feeling that you are making a financial mistake.

Ensure that your wants
are logical

Many years ago during a counseling session I had with job applicant, we took a break for lunch, and he drove me to a restaurant on the beach. He drove a truck, something unusual for an attorney, and en route I asked him why. "Money doesn't mean anything to me," he replied. "I don't have to work so I just do what I want. As a result I can't afford a big car so I drive this truck."

During lunch our counseling session continued, and he revealed that he had just been offered a job with great opportunity but had turned it down. When I asked why, he said that they were offering him only $27,500 and he felt he was "worth more than that."

I asked him how much he made at his last job, and he said $23,000. He was currently making less than $20,000. The reason he felt that he was worth more was because his friends all earned more than that. This is how many people judge their worth, but it's completely irrelevant unless the friends all have the same background, education, training, and experience. Here was a man who had never made more than $23,000 in his life turning down an attractive job offer for 20 percent more than he had ever made because it wasn't enough money.

Had I been interviewing him for a job, I probably would have dropped him right there. First he told me he didn't care about money, and then he said he turned down an attractive position solely because of money—an inherent inconsistency. Second, he had a grossly inflated value of himself based upon a false syllogism: My friends make more than $27,500; they are my friends; therefore I am worth more than $27,500.

The error of this reasoning is apparent. But it was not his faulty reasoning that would have spelled the coup de grâce for him with me. It was the inconsistency in his telling me how he disdained money, yet the sole reason he had for rejecting a fine offer was money.

You cannot base your salary upon what other people are making. For one reason, pay for the same job varies widely from company to company and from location to location. In 1991, the lowest pay for an administrative assistant/executive secretary was $1,602 a month in Bakersfield, California. The highest pay for the same job was $2,285 per month in Los Angeles. Lowest pay for a secretary was $1,286 in Temecula, California as opposed to the highest pay of $2,064 in Los Angeles. A receptionist with typing skills made $1,581 in San Francisco, but only $1,161 in Bakersfield.

You have a right to expect to be paid a reasonable salary and benefits in return for your work, and you shouldn't be shy about discussing them frankly and openly. But you must be pragmatic about what you want and what you feel you are worth. Don't worry about what your friends are making. That's irrelevant to what you should earn. Determine what **you** need, what **you** want, and what **you'll** settle for and know these three figures going in to the interview.

Women's Pay

Working women earn approximately 64 cents for every dollar earned by working men in the United Sates. Between 1947 and 1980 nearly 10 million more women than men entered the workforce and they came into it with little prior work experience. Research has shown that the education level of men in the workforce has risen faster than the education level of the female workforce. Evidently, for a variety of reasons, many more women than men have taken lower-paying jobs.

As a result, there is a growing controversy about the level of women's pay compared with men's. The theory of comparable worth has been developed to eliminate what many consider to be an insidious form of sex discrimination. A good example would be the disparity between the pay of nurses compared with the average doctor's remuneration.

Comparable worth, however, is a concept that is, at present, mostly talk, and not something you can rely upon. Some laws have been passed to make things more equal. The Equal Pay Act of 1963 ensures that women who perform the same work as men will receive the same pay. This covers employees engaged in commerce or the production of goods for commerce and includes all state and local government employees and most federal employees. But it does not cover work that is not the same.

Title VII of the Civil Rights Act of 1964 makes it unlawful to discriminate against any individual with respect to compensation, terms, conditions, or privileges of employment, because of such individual's . . . sex. Anyone complaining must prove that the employer's wage policy has a disproportionately adverse impact on a group protected under Title VII for disparate treatment or for disparate impact.

Lynn Weir, a Seattle attorney, summarizes how an aggrieved party can prove liability under Title VII:

> In a disparate treatment claim, a plaintiff seeks to prove that an employer intentionally treats some people less favorably than others because of their race, color, religion, sex or national origin. In a disparate impact claim, a plaintiff challenges employment practices that are facially neutral in their treatment of different groups

but that in fact fall more harshly on one group than another and cannot be justified by business necessity. To prevail on a disparate impact theory a plaintiff need not prove a discriminatory motive.

I include this very short and extremely superficial mention of Title VII so that you will realize that when your interview turns to a discussion of salary, you may still be at a disadvantage and that, even though there are laws that attempt to grant equal treatment, they are not perfect, nor do they adequately solve the problem of unequal pay.

What's important in the context of the job interview is that you are aware of the problem. How you handle it, whether you want to fight for equal rights and equal treatment as opposed to getting a job, regardless of whether or not a man doing similar work makes more, is up to you. The important thing is for you to **be prepared** for the difference. Even if you feel you're being treated unfairly, handle it as professionally as you can. Consistent with what I've said earlier, if you feel strongly about an issue such as this, it's much better to deal with it head on and express your emotions than to sublimate them. Just express them in an agreeable manner. No matter how firmly you speak, you should do it cordially.

Negotiation rules

Fred Allen once said that an agent's heart would fit in a flea's navel with room left over. Maybe, but that description wouldn't fit sports agent Bob Woolf. Woolf is an agent with ethics (quoting Arnold Glasgrow, "Don't part company with your ideals. They are anchors in a storm"). If money gets in the way of principle, Woolf lets his client go somewhere else. It is Woolf's emphasis on ethical behavior that makes him the best. He has a list of 101 rules on how to negotiate. They're listed in his excellent book, *Friendly Persuasion*, which you should read if you're negotiating salary. I'll just mention the more important rules here.

1. Try to get the other side to make the first offer. As we've mentioned, this is extremely important, because once you've mentioned what you want, you've almost certainly set a maximum on what you could get. And that maximum could be well below your interviewer's minimum! I can speak from experience. When I was a young lawyer in the early '70s, I had just resigned from Litton Industries to start my own practice and I was short of work. One day an executive with whom I had worked at Litton called. He had taken a new position as president of another major corporation, needed some legal help on the East Coast, and wondered if I was available for a few weeks. I said, sure. He asked how much he'd have to pay. I thought for awhile. He broke the silence by saying, "Don't hold me up, now." I figured what I had been making at Litton and quoted him $500 a week plus all my expenses, which was a lot more than I had been taking home at Litton. He didn't say much but told me to meet him at the plane in a couple of days for the trip east. I was happy. When I got to the plane, he said he had discussed my fee with his controller and neither thought that I should be paid so little, so they were going to pay me $700 per week. I later found out that they were expecting to pay between $1,000 and $1,500 per week.

2. Don't get angry because the offer isn't what you wanted, and

3. Determine how much room he has to move. Harken back to my earlier advice about needs and desires. If there's a big difference between the two, you've got plenty of room in which to negotiate. Further, their first offer is just that, an offer. You can diplomatically test the waters to see how firm they are.

4. Try to assess his weaknesses. Has the job been open very long? How many people have been interviewed? If they've been looking for awhile and have talked to a lot of people, this gives you a strong position because they are either very particular or the people they've interviewed haven't been interested. This means that they might need you more than you need them.

5. Assess your leverage. How unique are the job qualifications? How unique are your qualifications? If the job is one requiring specialized skill or qualifications and you have them, then your leverage is pretty high. If the job is one that could be done by a large number of people, and all they're looking for is a personality fit, your leverage is probably not too good. But if the person for whom you would be working is difficult to get along with and you have the unique ability to get along in a difficult personality mix, your leverage improves.

6. Make your presentation logically. When it gets down to actually talking numbers and you're far enough apart so that it's not a take-it-or-leave-it situation, you should be able to present your case as to why you're worth what you want in a cogent and reasonable manner. Lay out why you're worth it in terms of qualifications, personality, experience, and whatever other attributes you feel are relevant. But discuss each facet in turn. Don't shotgun the presentation, or the interviewer may think you're just talking off the top of your head, mentioning anything that floats in. It's much better to present each reason as a separate entity and discuss it rationally and fully before moving on to the next.

7. Start high but don't be ridiculous. As we've said, the theorem, "I want $X because my friends all make that much," won't get you very far. If you've done your preparation as I've suggested, you should have a good feel for the range that the job should pay. There's nothing wrong in asking for the top of the range, but if you ask for something that's so far out of line it's completely out of the question, you'll probably not be seriously considered any further, no matter how interested they were in you at first.

8. Don't give information, try to get information. Ah, this is where the skill of the interviewee comes to the foreground. If the interviewer broaches the question first by asking how much you want, you can easily turn the tables on him by asking him some questions about the job. You can rationally say that before you can arrive at that conclusion, you need to know more about what the job entails and how profitable the company or division or activity is. You can definitely ask what the company pays employees in similar positions, along with the salary range being considered. Resist, if you can, mentioning your needs or desires before you get this information.

9. Make sure the other side knows you want but don't need a job. Maybe that's not the case, but if your interviewer knows that you're in desperate straits, you almost totally destroy your negotiating position. You've got to appear to be looking, not begging. Remember that the interview is a two-way street. Not only are they interviewing you for a position, you're interviewing them to see if you **want** to work for them. If you can keep it on this level, you'll keep your negotiating posture on more even footing than you may feel it is.

10. Be flexible. If you present yourself in the light of "This is what I want and I'm not going to consider anything else," you are doing extreme damage to your interview. Not only will you risk getting the response of, "Well, thanks for coming in, but we can't afford that," you can give the impression of being intractable and stubborn, and this could result in an infavorable inference that could ruin the good you've done up until then. So learn how to present your desires in a friendly, non-confrontational manner, leaving yourself room to backtrack without losing face.

11. Keep a record of each conversation. I mentioned this earlier and it's vitally important. You might have many interviews with many different people or many interviews with the same person, and you don't want to be inconsistent. It's easy to forget what you've said and the numbers you've mentioned, especially if there's a substantial difference between your needs and your desires. So make as complete a record of each interview as soon as possible after the interview ends and be as detailed as possible.

12. Never raise or lower a price before you've been asked to do so. This might seem pretty elementary, but a sophisticated interviewer can make you feel like you want him to like you, so you may want to show your good faith by lowering your demand. This can be a big temptation, especially if negotiations have gone on for an extended period. It's like when you own a stock. When it goes up, and you should be considering selling, the urge is to hold; when it goes down, and you should be considering holding, the urge is to sell. So, too, in an interview. The urge is to reach agreement and you feel the best way to reach that agreement is to give a little. Don't do it unless you're prompted to by a request from the other side.

13. Don't give tit for tat. This is a corollary to the prior rule. If the person with whom you're negotiating comes up voluntarily, your impulse may be to come down an equal amount. Don't. There's no logical connection between how much your interviewer comes up and how much you come down. In fact, you don't have to come down **at all.** People sometimes think that in order to show good faith when the other side moves, you have to move. Not true and don't succumb to it. Perhaps a counter move by you is called for. But perhaps it's not. Whatever, a countermove by you is not automatically called for in response to a move by the other side.

14. Don't split the difference. Another corollary. You might be $X apart, and he offers to come up halfway if you'll come down half, so you think, "What the heck, let's get this over with." Or, "That's fair; he's giving and I'm giving and it's equal." But if you think about it, your interviewer has made a major mistake. He's already given you a number and raised it, and you haven't come down a penny! Woolf calls this a major point. "Don't snap at the bait, no matter how tempting it may be as a way to get nearly all you want and end the negotiation. Be a smart negotiator and you will earn a little more without offending anybody."

15. Don't let them intimidate you. You shouldn't have to think too much about this point. They wouldn't be negotiating salary with you if they were not very interested. So there's no way they can intimidate you if you always keep this truth uppermost in your mind during the negotiations.

16. Be patient. Unless they give you an ultimatum, you have plenty of time. No negotiation is much fun and you will almost always feel a self-imposed pressure to end it. Try to resist this feeling as much as you can. The negotiations will continue until you reach an impasse. That impasse will be reached when you've got them as high as they're going to go. When you know that, then you can make a decision. But they are the ones who need the employee, so, unless you're starving, you should view time as your ally, not theirs.

17. If you have what you want, don't let it go farther. Or, put another way, don't be greedy. While you don't want to accept less than their minimum, as I did years ago, if you've had fairly detailed negotiations and finally have what you want and need, take it and start work. If you prolong the negotiations, you run the risk of alienating them to the point where they might withdraw the offer, or, worse, they might find someone they want more than they want you.

18. Don't be afraid to leave something on the table. So what if you don't get the absolute maximum they might have been willing to pay? That's something you may never find out. And rather than risk losing an offer that would satisfy you for the hope of getting a few more dollars, it's better to grab what you want when you can get it and leave something on the table. If it's true that they got you for a little less than they were willing to pay, they'll feel they got a bargain and that can result in better treatment and a good atmosphere.

19. Don't ever burn your bridges. You never know when you might want to come back and ask for a job again. So if things don't work out, depart on a cordial note. Thank them for their time and interest. If they reject you, take it with good cheer. Put yourself in their place. It's not easy to turn someone down so this will leave a good taste in their mouth and you can never have too much goodwill. If you do the rejecting, do it as gently as possible with a good, cogent explanation and depart with thanks and in a friendly manner. As I said, sometime down the line, you could be looking for work there again.

20. Use common sense.

Vacation

Don't worry about asking about vacation. Employers do not expect their employees to work fifty-two weeks a year (they may want them to, but they don't expect it). Vacation is one of the most important elements of a job, and you should not shrink from asking about it. Most of the interviewers with whom I have spoken expect—and welcome—questions about vacation. You will not be jeopardizing receiving further consideration by letting the interviewer know that you are interested in the vacation and other job benefits. It's much better for you to ask about it before you receive an offer. Where are you if you take a job and then find out that you only get one day off a year? If you knew that before, it would probably have kept you from accepting an offer.

R.E. Taylor, vice president of personnel administration for the Bank of America, states a typical view: "It's not a negative to ask about vacation. It's our experience that it's very important to people today. When I applied for a job, I just wanted a job. We find that people's expectations are greater and more varied than they were. Leisure time is important to them. They're concerned about the environment and where they want to live and work. It's very important to them. We have people asking, 'Can I work downtown in the Towers? Can I work by the beach?' I don't think we can afford to have that type of question be a turnoff."

The general rule relating to vacations and benefits is that, like salary, they are items you should not bring up until the interviewer has raised the subject or has let you know that he is definitely interested in you. Once you have determined that, you should find out as much about the job—what it pays and what the responsibilities and benefits are—as you can.

CHECKLIST

★ Don't bring up the subject of salary yourself.

★ The interviewer won't want to discuss salary until he has made an initial determination that he is interested in you.

★ If it appears that the interview is ending with his expressing interest in seeing you again, then you can ask about salary.

★ If you raise the subject yourself, don't beat around the bush.

★ You must do research into yourself before you go into the interview.

★ Make a budget to determine how much money you must have.

★ Don't worry about what your friends are making.

★ Make a list of the things you have to offer an employer.

★ Try to find out what the job pays before you reveal your current salary.

★ Don't give the interviewer a copy of your tax return.

★ After he has revealed his interest in you, ask about vacation and benefits.

DISCRIMINATION

The law relating to what may and may not be asked during an interview is simple. Questions may not be asked for the purpose of discriminating on the basis of race, color, religion, sex, national origin, birthplace, age, or physical disability.

Federal laws don't expressly prohibit an interviewer from asking questions about your race, color, religion, or national origin, but the Equal Employment Opportunity Commission (EEOC) has issued a statement that it regards such inquiries with "extreme disfavor." It also says:

Except in those infrequent instances where religion or national origin is a bona fide occupational qualification reasonably necessary for the performance of a particular job, an applicant's race, religion and the like are totally irrelevant to his or her ability or qualifications as a prospective employee, and no useful purpose is served by eliciting such information. . . .

Accordingly, in the investigation of charges alleging the commission of unlawful employment practices the Commission will pay particular attention to the use by the party against whom charges have been made of pre-employment inquiries concerning race, religion, color, or national origin, or other inquiries which tend directly or indirectly to disclose such information. The fact that such questions are asked may, unless otherwise explained, constitute evidence of discrimination, and will weigh significantly in the Commission's decision as to whether or not [the law] has been violated.

Basically what you need to remember is that all questions should be job related. The United States Supreme Court has said that "the touchstone is business necessity."

State laws on the subject are more specific. Each state has laws relating to employment practices. They are generally known as fair employment practices laws and forbid employment bias based on race, color, sex, age, religion, national origin, birthplace, or physical disability.

Most states prohibit employers from asking questions that might prove prejudicial. California law, for instance, prohibits "any non-job-related inquiry, either verbal or through the use of an application form which directly or indirectly limits a person's employment opportunities because of race, color, religion, national origin, ancestry, medical condition (cancer related), physical handicap, marital status, sex, or age (40+)." Employers are to confine themselves to questions related to the applicant's qualifications for the job or potential for the job. It is all right to ask, "Do you have any physical condition or handicap which may limit your ability to perform the job applied for?"—but illegal to ask, "Do you have any physical disabilities or handicaps?" It is all right to ask if the job-seeker speaks a second language, but it is illegal to ask the applicant's mother tongue.

Most states publish lists of legal and illegal questions as a guideline for employees. Following are the lists for California and New York. For your state's list, contact the Fair Employment Practices Commission in your state. It may not be called that in each state (in New York, for instance, it's called the State Division of Human Rights), but a phone call to your nearest state employment office will guide you to the right office. If you have a question, don't hesitate to call your state office or the EEOC.

California

Pre-employment Inquiries

A list of acceptable and unacceptable inquiries employers may make prior to hiring an individual is reproduced below. The list has been issued by California's Department of Fair Employment and Housing.

The California Fair Employment Practice Act prohibits any non-job-related inquiry, either verbal or through the use of an application form, which directly or indirectly limits a person's employment opportunities because of race, color, religion, national origin, ancestry, medical condition (cancer related), physical handicap, marital status, sex, or age (40+). The regulations of the Fair Employment & Housing Commission define this to include any question which:

- Identifies a person on a basis covered by the Act.

or

- Results in the disproportionate screening out of members of a protected group.

or

- Is not a valid predictor of successful job performance.

It is the employer's right to establish job-related requirements and to seek the most qualified individual for the job. It is presumed that the information obtained through application forms and interviews is used by the employer in making selection and assignment decisions. For this reason, the employer should make only those inquiries necessary to determine the applicant's eligibility to be considered for employment. Documents required for legitimate purposes which reveal protected information (such as birth certificates, naturalization papers, or medical histories), may be requested at the point of hire, not before. (The point of hire is reached once the employer has decided to hire and so informs the applicant.)

This guide is not intended to be an exhaustive compilation of all acceptable and unacceptable inquiries. The examples listed are representative of questions fre-

181

Discrimination

quently asked. Those considered unacceptable are likely to limit the employment opportunities of persons protected by the FEP Act. For further detail, consult the Commission's Employment Regulations. These regulations and answers to questions on pre-employment inquiries can be obtained by writing to the Department of Fair Employment & Housing, 1201 I Street, Sacramento, CA 95814.

Collecting Applicant Flow Data

It is not unlawful for an employer to collect applicant-flow and other recordkeeping data for statistical purposes. Employers are encouraged to solicit this information on a voluntary basis in order to comply with federal and state requirements and for affirmative action efforts.

It is recommended that the material be collected on a separate form or tear-off portion of the application and be filed separately. Misuse of this data constitutes a violation of the FEP Act.

California

ACCEPTABLE	SUBJECT	UNACCEPTABLE
Name	**Name**	Maiden name.
"Have you ever used another name? / or / "Is any additional information relative to change of name, use of an assumed name, or nickname necessary to enable a check on your work and education record? If yes, please explain."		
Place of residence.	**Residence**	"Do you own or rent your home?"
Statement that hire is subject to verification that applicant meets legal age requirements.	**Age**	Age. Birthdate. Dates of attendance of completion of elementary or high school.
"If hired can you show proof of age?"		
"Are you over eighteen years of age?"		Questions which tend to identify applicants over age 40.
"If under eighteen, can you, after employment, submit a work permit?"		

"Can you, after employment, submit verification of you legal right to work in the United States?" / or/ Statement that such proof may be required after employment.	**Birthplace, Citizenship**	Birthplace of applicant, applicant's parents, spouse, or other relatives. "Are you a U.S. citizen?" / or/ Citizenship of applicant, applicant's parent, spouse, or other relatives. Requirements that applicant produce naturalization, first papers, or alien card *prior to employment.*
Languages applicant reads, speaks, or writes.	**National Origin**	Questions as to nationality, lineage, ancestry, national origin, descent, or parentage of applicant, applicant's parents, or spouse. "What is your mother tongue?" / or/ Language commonly used by applicant. How applicant acquired ability to read, write, or speak a foreign language.
Name and address of parent or guardian if applicant is a minor. Statement of company policy regarding work assignment of employees who are related.	**Sex, Marital status, Family**	Questions which indicate applicant's sex. Questions which indicate applicant's marital status. Number and/ or ages of children or dependents. Questions regarding pregnancy, child bearing, or birth control. Name or address of relative, spouse, or children of adult applicant. "With whom do you reside?" / or/ "Do you live with your parents?"
	Race, Color	Questions as to applicant's race or color. Questions regarding applicant's complexion or color of skin, eyes, hair.

Statement that photograph may be required after employment.	**Physical description, Photograph**	Questions as to applicant's height and weight.
		Require applicant to affix a photograph to application.
		Request application, at his or her option, to submit a photograph.
		Require a photograph after interview but before employment.
Statement by employer that offer may be made contingent on applicant passing a job-related physical examination. "Do you have any physical condition or handicap which may limit your ability to perform the job applied for? If yes, what can be done to accommodate your limitation?"	**Physical condition, Handicap**	Questions regarding applicant's general medical conditions, state of health, or illnesses. Questions regarding receipt of Workers' Compensation. "Do you have any physical disabilities or handicaps?"
Statement by employer of regular days, hours, or shifts to be worked.	**Religion**	Questions regarding applicant's religion. Religious days observed / or/ "Does your religion prevent you from working weekends or holidays?"
"Have you ever been convicted of a felony, or, within (specified time period) a misdemeanor which resulted in imprisonment?" (Such a question must be accompanied by a statement that a conviction will not necessarily disqualify applicant from the job applied for.)	**Arrest, Criminal record**	Arrest record / or/ "Have you ever been arrested?"
Statement that bonding is a condition of hire.	**Bonding**	Questions regarding refusal or cancellation of bonding.

Questions regarding relevant skills acquired during applicant's U.S. military service.	**Military service**	General questions regarding military services such as dates, and type of discharge.
		Questions regarding service in a foreign military.
	Economic status	Questions regarding applicant's current or past assets, liabilities, or credit rating, including bankruptcy or garnishment.
"Please list job-related organizations, clubs, professional societies, or other associations to which you belong—you may omit those which indicate your race, religious creed, color, national origin, ancestry, sex, or age."	**Organizations, activities**	"List all organizations, clubs, societies, and lodges to which you belong."
"By whom were you referred for a positon here?"	**References**	Questions of applicant's former employers or acquaintances which elicit information specifying the applicant's race, color, religious creed, national origin, ancestry, physical handicap, medical condition, marital status, age, or sex.
Names of persons willing to provide professional and/ or character references for applicant.		
Name and address of person to be notified in case of accident or emergency.	**Notice in case of emergency**	Name and address of relative to be notified in case of accident or emergency.

New York

SAMPLE QUESTIONS

APPLICATION FOR EMPLOYMENT

Personal Information

Date
Social Security Number
Name
Present Address
Permanent Address
Phone No.
If related to anyone in our employment, state name and department
Referred By

Employment Desired

Position
Date you can start
Are you employed now?
If so, may we inquire of your present employer?
Have you ever applied to this company before? Where? When?

Education

Name and location of school } *(For grammar school, high school,*
Did you graduate? } *college, trade, business or correspon-*
Subjects studied } *dence school)*

Subjects of special study or research work
What foreign languages do you speak fluently? Read? Write?
Activities (You may exclude those which indicate the race, creed, sex,
  marital status, age, color, national origin, or physical handicap of its
  members.)

Former Employers

Date (From/ To)
Name and Address of employer } *(List employers, starting with*
Position } *the most recent.)*
Reason for leaving

References

Name
Address
Business
Years Acquainted

Other

In case of emergency notify (name, address, phone no.)

I authorize investigation of all statements contained in this application.

I understand that misrepresentation or omission of facts called for is cause for dismissal.

Signature and date

Pre-employment Inquiries

The following Rulings on Inquiries were reflected in a pamphlet issued by the state Division of Human Rights on August 1, 1988.

Directly Revelatory Inquiries

The Law expressly prohibits employers[1a], employment agencies, landlords, and real estate sellers, brokers and salespersons, and creditors from asking certain questions either in an application form or in a personal interview before selecting an employee, apprentice or tenant or making a real estate sale or lease, or extending credit. The following are examples of different types of inquiries that have been ruled lawful or unlawful:

Subject	Lawful[2]	Unlawful
Age	Are you 18 years of age or older? If not, state your age.[3]	How old are you? What is your date of birth? What are the ages of your children, if any?
Arrest Record	Have you ever been convicted of a crime? (Give details)[4]	Have you ever been arrested?
Birth control	None	Inquiry as to capacity to reproduce, advocacy of any form of birth control or family planning.
Disability[5]	None	Do you have a disability? Have you ever been treated for any of the following diseases . . . ? Do you have now, or have had, a drug or alcohol problem?

[1a] Polygraph testing: Inquiries which are unlawful when made by employers are also unlawful when made by polygraph testers as agents for employers.

A new federal law, effective 12/27/ 88, bans most employer use of polygraph tests. It bars pre-hiring polygraph screening and random testing and sets strict rules gov-

187

erning administration of polygraph tests to employees suspected of a particular wrongdoing. There are few exceptions from this ban in the law signed by the President on June 27, 1988.

[2] See Section 6, Disparate Impact Inquiries.

[3] Effective January 1, 1985 for public employers and January 1, 1986 for private employers, the maximum age limit for age discrimination purposes has been removed.

[4] An applicant may not be denied employment because of a conviction record unless there is a direct relationship between the offense and the job or unless hiring would be an unreasonable risk. An ex-offender denied employment is entitled to a statement of the reasons for such denial. Correction Law, Article 22-A, Sec. 754.

[5] The HRL now extends coverage to those individuals who either have a record of a disabling condition or who are regarded by others as being disabled. See definition of disability, infra.

(It is UNLAWFUL to inquire, either directly or indirectly, about an applicant's/ employee's disabilities. An employer may inquire only whether a prospective employee can perform specific tasks in a reasonable manner. An employer may not disqualify an applicant/ employee because of suspected FUTURE risk to his/ her health of performing a specific job.)

The above limitations apply equally to questions which may be asked of an employee who applies for or is under consideration for promotion, transfer, upgrading, etc.

They also apply equally to questions asked by a prospective employer, either orally, by telephone, in writing or otherwise, of a former employer, with reference to an applicant or a person under consideration for employment.

Subject	Lawful[7]	Unlawful
Marital Status	None	Do you wish to be addressed as Miss? Mrs.? Ms.? Are you married? Single? Divorced? Separated?
Marital Status	None	Name or other information about spouse
National Origin	None	Inquiry into applicant's lineage, ancestry, national origin, descent, parentage or nationality. Nationality of applicant's parents or spouse

Race or Color	None	Complexion or color of skin. Coloring.
Religion or Creed	None	Inquiry into applicant's religious denomination, religious affiliations, parish or church, religious holidays observed. Applicant may not be told "This is a (Catholic, Protestant or Jewish) organization."[6]
Sex	None	Inquiry as to gender.

[6] Sec., 296(11). Nothing contained in this section shall be construed to bar any religious or denominational institution or organization or any organization organized for charitable purposes, which is operated, supervised or controlled by or in connection with a relgious organization, from limiting employment or sales or rental of housing accommo- dations or admission to or giving preference to persons of the same religion or denomination or from making such selection as is calculated by such organization to promote the religious principles for which it is established or maintained.

[7] See Section 6, Disparate Impact Inquiries, infra.

Indirectly Revelatory Inquiries

It is unlawful to ask questions the answers to which will indirectly reveal information as to race, creed, color, national origin, sex, marital status, disability, age or arrest record in cases where such information may not be asked directly. In making such rulings, the Division has applied a rule of reason, taking into account the need for the information asked as well as the danger that it will reveal other information that should not be considered in selection.

The following are Division rulings on inquiries indirectly revelatory of race, creed, color, national origin, sex, marital status, disability, or age:

Subject	Lawful	Unlawful
Address or Duration of Residence	Applicant's place of residence. How long a resident of this state or city?	

Birthdate	None	Requirements that applicant submit birth certficate, naturalizatioon or baptismal record.
		Requirement that applicant produce proof of age in form of birth certificate or baptismal record.
Birthplace	None	Birthplace of applicant.
		Birthplace of applicant's parents, spouse, or other close relatives.
Citizenship	Are you a citizen of the United States? If not a citizen of the United States, do you intend to become a citizen of the United States? If you are not a United States citizen, have you the legal right to remain permanently in the United States? Do you intend to remain permanently in the United States?	Of what country are you a citizen? Whether an applicant is naturalized or a native-born citizen; the date when the applicant acquired citizenship.
		Requirement that · applicant produce naturalization papers or first papers.
		Whether applicant's parents or spouse are naturalized or native-born citizens of the United States; the date when such parents or spouse acquired citizenship.
Driver's License	Do you possess a valid NYS driver's license?	Requirement that applicant produce a driver's license.
Education	Inquiry into applicant's academic, vocational or professional education and the public and private schools attended.	

Experience	Inquiry into work experience.	
Language	Inquiry into languages applicant speaks or writes fluently.	What is your native language? Inquiry into how applicant acquired ability to read, write or speak a foreign language.
Military Experience	Inquiry into applicant's military experience in the Armed Forces of the United States or in a State Militia.	Inquiry into applicant's military experience other than in the Armed Forces or the United States in a State Militia.
	Inquiry into applicant's service in particular branch of United States Army, Navy, etc. Did you receive a dishonorable discharge.[8]	Did you receive a discharge from the military in other than honorable circumstances?
Name	Have you ever worked for this company under a different name? Is additional information relative to change of name, use of an assumed name or nickname necessary to enable a check on your work record? If yes, please explain.	Original names of an applicant whose name has been changed by court order or otherwise. Maiden name of a married woman. If you have ever worked under another name, state name and address.
Notice in Case of Emergency	None	Name and address of person to be notified in case of an accident or emergency.
Organizations	Inquiry into applicant's membership in organizations which the applicant considers relevant to his or her ability to perform the job.	ist all clubs, societies and lodges to which you belong.

| Photograph | None | Requirement or option that applicant affix a photograph to employment form at any time before hiring. |
| Relatives | Name of applicant's relatives already employed by the company | Number, names, addresses and ages of applicant's spouse, children or relatives not employed by the company. |

[8] Inquiries regarding military service should be accompanied by a statement that a dishonorable discharge is not an absolute bar to employment and that other factors will affect a final decision.

[9] This inquiry (as well as those related to age and marital status) may be asked after a person has been hired.

Disparate Impact Inquiries

Selection criteria which are facially neutral in their treatment of different groups but which impact more severely on one protected group and cannot be justified by business necessity are unlawful.

Thus, inquiries which would otherwise be deemed lawful may, in certain circumstances, be deemed as evidence of unlawful discrimination when the inquiry seeks to elicit information about a selection criterion which has a disproportionately burdensome effect and the criterion is not job related. Such criteria may not be used as a basis for selecting employees, apprentices or tenants or as a basis for deciding whether to make a real estate sale or lease. The inquirer may justify the making of such inquiry by the showing of a business necessity.

Other legal protections

Of course, there are laws that protect job applicants other than those relating to pre-employment inquiries. For example, the New York Human Rights Law prohibits employers from refusing to employ persons with disabilities that are unrelated to job performance. One woman who was 5 feet

6 inches tall and weighed 249 pounds was offered a job by Xerox subject to passing a pre-employment medical examination. The examining physician found her medically unacceptable because of her obesity, and she was refused employment. Xerox argued that obesity was not a present impairment but that it could refuse to hire the obese because of a statistical likelihood that obesity would produce impairments in the future and have an adverse impact on disability and life insurance programs. The woman was a widow and had raised five children after her husband died; she argued that her obesity constituted a disability, but never prevented her from performing any task. The New York Court of Appeals held that her obesity constituted an impairment and awarded her monetary damages for mental anguish and humiliation, plus back pay and a position at Xerox.

Age discrimination

One extremely sensitive area involving unlawful pre-employment inquiries involves age. People over forty often have a difficult time finding jobs simply because of their age even though the law specifically prohibits age discrimination. A job-seeker who happens to be female, in addition to being over forty, can feel as if she's starting out with two strikes against her. One forty-five-year-old woman attorney told me a story that epitomizes this problem and the way age discrimination can rear its ugly head when you least expect.

> I was on my third interview with one of the largest firms in Sacramento. At that point I thought I was a shoo-in. I had to interview an older man who was on their management committee. We were talking about housing in Sacramento and where I would live. I mentioned that I'd like to live near my daughter because she would soon be moving to Germany with her husband.
>
> He said, "Oh, you probably want to move up here so you can baby-sit your grandchildren." Then he paused and said, "Well, do you have any grandchildren?"

I did, but I smiled and said, "Well, I really don't think that's relevant" or something to that effect. It made me really uneasy because if I don't tell him he's going to feel like I'm going to be uncooperative and secretive to work with. And if I do tell him, there's definitely a stigma attached to being a grandparent, and he's going to think I'll fall asleep in the afternoon, that I can't handle a regular fifty-hour work week. Because I didn't answer the question I felt I was being uncooperative.

Discriminatory questions in an interview are insidious and this story shows how damaging they can be to an interviewee who is unprepared and/or does not know the law. Even if you know the law, as this woman did, being asked a question that probes prohibited areas can be devastating. The problem is that you're placed in a difficult position, as this woman so eloquently described. If you answer the question, you might be revealing information that could result in your losing an offer. If you don't answer it, you risk appearing uncooperative. If you challenge the question, you might appear argumentative.

How to respond to an unlawful question

When you are asked a question that you feel must be challenged, you should deal with it head on, immediately. That said, however, one point that I've hammered away at is that *most* selection interviewers are *unsophisticated*. They don't ask predetermined questions. They will ask you whatever pops into their heads. So they may ask you if you're religious because they are religious and wonder if you go to the same church or temple. In this event, it would have nothing to do with whether or not they're going to hire you. Or you may be asked the derivation of your name because the interviewer (and for the balance of this chapter, let's assume the interviewer is a woman) thinks you're nervous and this would be something you could talk about freely, not because you look Estonian and the interviewer hates all Estonians. Remember, for the most part, the interviewer is simply trying to find out what kind of a person you are and whether she has a good feeling about you. So your best option in most cases, assuming your reply can't hurt you, is to answer the question, ignore the possibility of unlawful pre-employment inquiry, and go on with the interview.

But if the question bothers you, and you feel that the interviewer knows she's out of bounds, answer the question, but let the interviewer know that you know the law. One way to do it is to ask her if the question is an appropriate or lawful question to be asked in a job interview. This puts the onus on the interviewer to defend the question. But, if you feel uncomfortable with the question and at the same time feel that your answer could hurt you, trust your feelings, decline to answer, and tell the interviewer of your feelings, in as non-threatening a mode as possible, and put the interviewer on notice that you are aware of the law and that she has entered a protected area. This is especially important if you feel your answer could cost you an offer, as the woman in the age discrimination story felt.

However, her method of handling it, by stating that she didn't think the question was "relevant" doesn't do the job. Far better to ask the interviewer if it's legal, which transfers the burden of defending the question to the interviewer and removes the onus of declining to answer from your shoulders. This also effectively challenges the legality of the question. "Relevance" and "legality" are two entirely different matters: there's nothing in the law that prohibits an interviewer from asking an irrelevant question. An easy way to challenge the legality of the question is to use a significant key word in asking the interviewer about the question. "Appropriate," is good. "Legal" is better. "Lawful" uses the terminology of most legislation.

In the end, if you can, you should give the interviewer the benefit of the doubt and go on with the interview as if nothing untoward had happened. If you're firm (but polite) in your position on not answering the prohibited inquiry, it's essential that you continue the interview on the same gracious tone that was present prior to the introduction of the discriminatory matter. By acting in such a professional manner, you accomplish one of two things. If the interviewer asked the question innocently, you will convey the impression that you don't hold any grudges, recognize that anyone can make a mistake, and are willing to accept her, regardless of her mistake. If she asked it intentionally this gives you the upper hand. Since you've shown that you know the law and that she's violated it, your interviewer has to worry about your making an issue out of it. If nothing else, from that point on in the interview, she should be reluctant to introduce any further discriminatory matter.

Handling an illegal pre-employment inquiry is never easy. But, as with other problems that can arise in an interview, if you're prepared for it you will be in much better shape to handle it in the event it arises.

Filing claims

If you really think you've been treated unfairly and you don't get an offer you want, then you should feel free to file a claim with the state and the EEOC. But think about it and be sure that you really feel in your heart that you were discriminated against. Don't just file a charge on a whim or out of pique because you didn't get an offer. And don't file unless you have a legitimate complaint. **The question must have been asked for the purpose of discriminating against you because of an illegal reason or have the effect of discriminating against you.** This may not be easy to determine, although an interviewer who asked such a question may have difficulty explaining why she asked it if not to make a hire-no hire decision based upon your answer. Still, the simplest thing to do is to chalk it all up to experience and go on to your next interview.

If you feel you were asked a prohibited pre-employment inquiry and, as a result, were discriminated against, and want to pursue the matter, you should file a charge within the applicable filing period. You should file concurrently with both your state agency and the EEOC. The filing periods in the various states vary, so you should contact your state agency to determine what it is. The filing period in California (and in approximately 75 percent of the states) is 300 days. The EEOC filing period is 180 days or the period allowed by the state in which the alleged violation occurred, whichever is longer. As a matter of procedure, the EEOC will defer until the state agency has investigated and taken action; then the EEOC will investigate after the state agency deferral has ended.

After the EEOC conducts an investigation, it will make a determination to see if there is reasonable cause to believe that your charge is true. Although the EEOC is making an effort to reduce its backlog of charges, it currently may take years to institute an investigation. If you wish to proceed against the employer sooner, you may request a notice to sue anytime after you file your charge with the EEOC. If the EEOC investigates, you will not take part in the investigation, and you do not need an attorney. All of the EEOC's investigation is confidential. All you'll find out is whether the EEOC has determined if there is reasonable cause to believe your charge is true. If the EEOC does not find such a reasonable cause, it will advise you of this and of your "right to sue" in court.

If the EEOC does find reasonable cause, it will attempt to conciliate the matter by meeting with the potential employer and reaching an agreement on the remedy. If no agreement is reached, the EEOC may file a suit or it may issue you a "right to sue" letter. You have 90 days after receipt of a "right to sue" letter from the EEOC to file your own suit.

If you don't have an attorney, the courts are authorized to appoint one for you and to start the action without payment of a filing fee. Just because the EEOC does not find reasonable cause does not mean that you can't file a suit yourself, and it doesn't mean that you won't recover.

If you can afford an attorney, you should retain your own. But if you can't, it has been held that all you have to do is file your "right to sue" letter in federal court and apply for the appointment of counsel. If you do these things within the 90-day period after receipt of your "right to sue" letter, you should be safe in having preserved your cause of action.

However, according to EEOC counsel Steven Gaffin, "courts are not overly generous" in appointing attorneys for applicants. The United States District Court for the Central

District of California requires that a lawsuit be filed and an application in forma pauperis, which describes permission given to a poor person to sue without liability for costs.

The remedies you can hope to receive if you get a favorable judgment from the court can include attorney's fees. So if you retain your own attorney and win, the employer may have to pay your attorney. Of course you can also get damages. For example, perhaps you can prove that you were not hired because of discrimination. If the job for which you were interviewing paid $20,000 per year and you were out of work for a year thereafter and couldn't get a job despite diligent effort, the court could award you $20,000 in damages. State and local governments are **not** immune from paying salary and attorney's fees in cases of prohibited discrimination.

While you may be awarded your attorney's fees if you win, you might have to pay the other party's attorney's fees if you lose. Although this is very rare, it has happened and it is something of which you should be aware.

Now that you have a general idea of what your rights are, you must put this knowledge in the context of everything else you've learned in this book. Remember that the inquiry must have been asked for the purpose of discriminating against you for an unlawful reason. Beyond that, the question is whether you have the energy and the time to follow through. Perhaps the better course would be to move on to the next interview—you wouldn't have been happy working under those circumstances anyway.

Applications

Reader Michael Rezendes of Ventura, California, expresses a frustration with the application part of the screening interview:

> During my job hunting activities, I have been continually confronted with and frustrated by job application forms. These pesky forms seem to continually be a stumbling block in my efforts to

conduct effective interviews . . . They force you to reveal your lia-
bilities, your limited experience, gaps in your job record, reasons
for leaving jobs, references, and past earnings very early in the
interview process.

Frequently by the time I have filled out the application I feel
totally demoralized and feel I couldn't possibly have a chance at
the job or conduct an effective interview. It seems unless you have
a near perfect job history or background these application forms
tear you to shreds right before the upcoming interview. Especially
frustrating is when you show up for an interview and are handed
an application to fill out before the interview or before seeing anyone. Usually I end up filling it out because I don't know what else
to do.

The rules for pre-employment inquiries are equally pertinent to applications. (Refer to the "sample questions" listed
as acceptable by the California Department of Fair Employment and Housing earlier in this chapter.) Filling out an
application is much easier, however, because you have total
control and time to think and plan.

Just because you are presented with a form to fill out
does not mean that you have to answer all the questions on
it. Take it from me, forms that contain questions or terms
and conditions are not written in concrete. You can alter
them before signing them, or decline to answer parts of
them. What you must realize is that those forms have been
drafted by highly paid lawyers. Each word is important or
it wouldn't be in there. And you can bet that there isn't
anything in there that is drafted with your interests in mind.

I know whereof I speak because, as an attorney for Litton Industries, I drafted the terms and conditions that were
put on the back of our vendors' purchase order forms. I
drafted the most onerous terms and conditions anyone's
ever seen. They protected Litton from here to Timbuktu
and back again. Still, 90 percent of the vendors would just
sign off on them without questioning anything. If anyone
questioned them, we would negotiate something that was
acceptable to both sides.

So when you see a preprinted application that contains
questions or terms and conditions, read it all and read it
slowly and thoroughly. If you don't like something, don't
answer the offending question, or alter the section you don't

like. Remember **EVERYTHING'S NEGOTIABLE.** How negotiable depends upon your negotiating position, of course, and that's something only you can determine.

Following is a sample application taken from Matthew Bender's *Employment Law Deskbook,* which was written to advise lawyers who advise employers on how to comply with the law. Because it was prepared for use by attorneys, you can safely presume that nothing in it is prohibited by law. This is an excellent form for use by **employers.** It looks like something I might draft if I were the attorney for an employer because it definitely protects my client. But that doesn't mean it would be in your best interests to answer all the questions and sign it. A form drafted for an employer is not one drafted with an employee's interests in mind. There's probably at least one provision that could easily redound to your disfavor. In fact, there are *many* areas of this application to which I would object.

XYZ COMPANY
An Equal Opportunity Employer
EMPLOYMENT APPLICATION

NAME: _____ S.S.No. _____
    First   Middle   Last
PRESENT ADDRESS: _____
_____
PREVIOUS ADDRESS: _____
_____
TELEPHONE NUMBER (Home) _____ (Business) _____
    Positon(s) Applied For: 1._____.
                        2._____
                        3._____

Full Time_____ Part Time_____ Temporary_____
Specify Days and Hours For Which You Are Available: _____
_____
Date Available: _____ Desired Salary: _____
Are you willing to relocate? Yes____ No____ If yes, specify location(s)
_____
How were you referred to the XYZ Company? _____
Are you authorized to work in the United States? Yes_____ No_____
(If you are a resident alien, please give your alien number on your
Resident Alien Card (Form I-551) _____).
Have you ever applied here before?   Yes__ No__If yes, specify the
date(s): _____

Have you been employed here before?   Yes__ No__If yes, specify the date(s): _____

Give the names and relationships of any relatives you have working for XYZ Company: _____

_____

Describe any impairments, physical or mental, that would interfere with your ability to perform the position(s) for which you are applying:

_____

Have you ever been convicted of a criminal offense? Yes_____ No_____
If Yes, please explain: _____

Are you at least 18 years of age? _____Yes _____No
Employment History:
    Start with your current or most recent employer.
1.   Employer: _____
     Address: _____

     Phone Number: _____
     Job Title: _____   Supervisor: _____
     Salary: _____
     Duties Performed: _____
     Reason for Leaving: _____
2.   Employer: _____
     Address: _____

     Phone Number: _____
     Job Title: _____   Supervisor: _____
     Salary: _____
     Duties Performed: _____
     Reason for Leaving: _____
3.   Employer: _____
     Address: _____

     Phone Number: _____
     Job Title: _____   Supervisor: _____
     Salary: _____
     Duties Performed: _____
     Reason for Leaving: _____
            If you need additional space, please continue
                on a separate sheet of paper.
Have you worked under a different name for any of these employers?
Yes_____ No_____ If yes, please identify the employer and state the
name: _____

_____

U.S. Military Record:

Have you served in the United States Armed Forces? _____Yes _____No   If yes, please give the dates of service:

From_____ To_____ Branch:_____

If you have a handicap or are a disabled veteran and would like to be considered under our Affirmative Action Program, please so indicate. (You need not provide us with this information if you do not wish to do so. If you choose to provide the information, it will be kept confidential except that your supervisors may be informed regarding work restrictions or accomodations that may be appropriate, and first aid people may be advised of possible emergency treatment.) _____Yes _____No If yes, describe any special skills you may have and any special adaptations needed because of the handicap. _____

PLEASE READ CAREFULLY BEFORE
SIGNING THIS APPLICATION

I authorize the Company to investigate all statements in this application and to secure any necessary information from all my employers, references, and academic institutions. I hereby release all of those employers, references, academic institutions, and the Company from any and all liability arising from their giving or receiving information about my employment history, my academic credentials or qualifications, and my suitability for employment with the Company. I also authorize the Company to secure financial and credit information through an appropriate agency, and I understand that, upon my written request made within a reasonable period of time, the agency providing a consumer credit report to the Company will provide me with a complete description of the nature and scope of the credit report investigation.

I understand that any offer of employment is contigent upon receipt of a satisfactory report concerning my credit, academic credentials, and employment references. I further understand that any false or misleading statements will be sufficient cause for rejection of my application if the Company has not employed me and for immediate dismissal if the Company has employed me. I also authorize the Company to supply information about my employment record, in whole or in part, in confidence to any prospective employer, government agency, or any other party having a legal and proper interest, and I hereby release the Company from any and all liability for its providing this information.

In the event of my employment with the Company, I will comply with all rules, regulations, and policies set forth in the Company's policy manual or other communications distributed by the Company.

I understand that nothing in this employment application, in the Company's policy statements or personnel guidelines, or in my communications with any Company official is intended to create an employment contract between the Company and me. I also understand that the Company has the right to modify its policies without giving me any notice of the changes. No promises regarding employment have been made to me, and I understand that no such promise of guarantee is binding upon the Company unless it is made in writing and signed by a Company officer. I understand that if an employment relationship is established, I have the right to terminate my employment at any time for any reason. I also understand that the Company retains the right to terminate my employment for any reason.

I hereby acknowledge that I have read and understand the preceding statement.

_____   _____

Signature of Applicant   Date

Social security numbers.   There are probably two reasons why this is asked for on the application. First, if you go to work for them your employer will have legal entitlement to possession of your social security number. Second, it's on the application so they can do a credit check on you. I never give anybody my social security number unless there's a legal entitlement to it. And the only people who have a legal entitlement to your social security number are people who will be paying you, so they can file the necessary tax reports. Nobody else has a legal right to your social security number.

However, that said, you should know that by not providing my social security number I do miss out on some things. For example, at least once I was refused the right to apply for an apartment because I would not divulge my social security number. I felt that protecting the confidentiality of my social security number was more important than the apartment. You might not think it is more important than getting a job. It's a value judgment that each person must make.

Don't be misled into believing promises of confidentiality. The Federal Reserve, an agency of the United States Government, requires the social security number of holders of federal reserve bills, notes, and bonds, and quotes the law as to confidentiality and promises confidentiality. Despite this, the Federal Reserve puts the recipient's social security number on the face of the envelopes when it mails interest checks. I've protested and quoted the law to the Federal Reserve, but it denies that this is a breach of confidentiality, and blithely continues to expose the social security numbers of all holders of Federal Reserve instruments for all the world to see on the face of the envelopes.

I would advise you to tell the interviewer that you'll supply the number if you accept an offer and become their employee. If they say that they won't process your application without it, you'll just have to make a judgment as to the importance of the confidentiality of your social security number. I'd estimate that more than 99 percent of the people disclose it with no worry and no problem. It is a lawful pre-employment inquiry in California.

Blanket release to your prior employers. I wouldn't agree to any language releasing a third party. That's the third party's problem. If the third party is worried about what they might reveal about you, then they can contact you for your release. If they do contact you, ask to see a copy of what they propose to reveal *before* you grant your release. If you don't like what they propose to reveal you can deny your release. You may provide your consent to allow any prior employer to provide information to the company, but under no circumstances should you sign any language that purports to *release* your prior employer from liability. That's no legitimate concern of your interviewer. There's a big difference between *consenting* to your prior employer's providing information and *releasing* your prior employer from any liability for any damages resulting from the release of false or defamatory information. You should recognize this difference and, if asked to sign such a statement, explain to your interviewer why you will sign the consent but not a release and why it's unfair for them to ask you to sign a release. Just hone in on the difference between a *consent* and a *release*. Maybe without your consent a former employer won't provide information, so you sign the consent. But a former employer who damages you should be liable for the damage done as a result of false or defamatory information, which is why you don't want to sign a release.

Credit check authorization. If you are asked to authorize a credit check you should ask for an exact copy of your credit report, not, as the application puts it, "a complete description of the nature and scope of the credit report investigation." The reason that this specific language is used is that the Federal Fair Credit Report Act only requires an employer to notify the applicant that such a report might be requested and to disclose information about its "nature and scope." So this consent only obligates the interviewer to comply with the *minimum* requirements of the law. There's no reason why you shouldn't be given an exact copy of the credit report. If you demand it as a condition to signing the consent, then the employer is required to provide you with it, regardless of the minimal requirements of the law. And the employer cannot correctly state that the law *prohibits* it from doing more simply because the law does not *require* it to do more. If you *don't* demand an exact copy in writing in your consent, you will have no enforceable right to receive it.

False information. I wouldn't agree to any stipulations that the company could dismiss me on the grounds of false information supplied by third parties. It's understandable that they might want you to agree to the right to dismiss you for false information supplied by you, but not for false information supplied by a third party beyond your control. I would not agree to the company's right to dismiss me for information that is "misleading." The term "misleading" is ambiguous and could mean anything. I would also delete the word "immediate" and request that in the event of any alleged false information I be given notice and the right to respond prior to any dismissal. You don't want to give your employer carte blanche to terminate you without being given a right to defend yourself.

Confidentiality. I wouldn't give the company authorization to supply information about me to anybody. That has nothing to do with your application for a job with them. It's important to your privacy that you control information disseminated about you to third parties. Nor would I agree to the release provision regarding the company providing information for the same reasons enumerated above.

Finally, I'd modify the provision that the company can change its policies without notifying me by adding the proviso "so long as it doesn't affect me or my job." And I'd limit their right to terminate me "for any reason" to "for any reason allowed by law."

The following example shows the sort of modifications to the fine print that I would make if this were my application. If you make changes in a document, do it in ink and initial each alteration. Two final caveats. When you sign something, initial each page. That way pages can't be substituted without your knowledge. Finally, ALWAYS GET, AND KEEP, A COMPLETE COPY OF ANYTHING YOU SIGN!!!! Otherwise you'll have no record of what you signed and won't know what your rights are in the event of a dispute.

PLEASE READ CAREFULLY BEFORE
SIGNING THIS APPLICATION

I authorize the Company to investigate all statements in this application and to secure any necessary information from all my employers, references, and academic institutions. ~~I hereby release all of those employers, references, academic institutions, and the Company from any and all liability arising from their giving or receiving information about my employment history, my academic credentials or qualifications, and my suitability for employment with the Company.~~ I also authorize the Company to secure financial and credit information through an appropriate agency, and I understand that, upon my written request made within a reasonable period of time, the agency providing a consumer credit report to the Company will provide me with a ~~complete description of the nature and scope~~ of the credit report investigation. *{ full and complete copy }*

I understand that any offer of employment is contingent upon receipt of a satisfactory report concerning my credit, academic credentials, and employment references. I further understand that any false ~~or misleading~~ statements *{ of a material nature made by me }* will be sufficient cause for rejection of my application if the Company has not employed me and for immediate dismissal if the Company has employed me. ~~I also authorize the Company to supply information about my employment record, in whole or in part, in confidence to any prospective employer, government agency, or any other party having a legal and proper interest, and I hereby release the Company from any and all liability for its providing this information.~~ *{ after being given adequate and reasonable prior notice and the prior right to respond to all allegations made against me. }*

In the event of my employment with the Company, I will comply with all rules, regulations, and policies set forth in the Company's policy manual or other communications distributed by the Company.

I understand that nothing in this employment application, in the Company's policy statements or personnel guidelines, or in my communications with any Company official is intended to create an employment contract between the Company and me. I also understand that the Company has the right to modify its policies without giving me any notice of the changes. *{ that do not affect me or my job }* No promises regarding employment have been made to me, and I understand that no such promise of guarantee is binding upon the Company unless it is made in writing and signed by a Company officer. I understand that if an employment relationship is established, I have the right to terminate my employment at any time for any reason. I also understand that the Company retains the right to terminate my employment for any reason. *{ allowed by law }*

I hereby acknowledge that I have read and understand the preceding statement.

_____   _____

Signature of Applicant   Date

Privacy and confidentiality

Although there is not a specific right of privacy in the United States Constitution, many states have amended their constitutions to provide its citizens with a fundamental right of privacy. California amended its constitution in 1972 by a vote of the people to provide:

> All people are by nature free and independent and have inalienable rights. Among these are enjoying and defending life and liberty, acquiring, possessing, and protecting property, and pursuing and obtaining safety, happiness, and privacy.

Personnel records. The right to privacy has been interpreted by California courts to provide employees with the right to be free from intrusion into certain personal affairs and the right to have the contents of many records maintained on the employee kept secret. So a former employer would probably be prohibited from disclosing information from your personnel file without your prior permission.

Letters of reference. Many states have defined letters of reference broadly to protect them from inspection without your permission. The definition in California has been interpreted to include any confidential information concerning qualification for employment, promotion, additional compensation, termination, or other disciplinary action.

AIDS. Some states, including California, prohibit employers from using the results of an AIDS blood test or information relating to AIDS research in any way for the determination of the suitability of employment.

Pre-employment testing

There are a number of conditions that may be attached to the screening phase of your job search. For instance, on the application form you may be asked to agree to submit to a physical exam or to sign a release for previous employment records. If you have reservations about any such conditions, you should either cross them out on the application form, or alter the wording to protect yourself, as I discussed above. But if you do this, you need to be prepared to discuss your reasoning when you get into the interview situation.

Drug and alcohol tests. Many employers will want to know if you use drugs, have used drugs, or are a potential drug user, and you may be asked in the interview or on the application if you would be willing to submit to testing.

The problem is that many of the tests for drugs are inaccurate. How can you protect against a false reading or a false conclusion? It would be a disaster if a urinalysis or check of your hair (don't laugh, this is one of the tests) shows that you use drugs.

Even if you don't use drugs or alcohol, you should be wary of invasive tests because of their potential for inaccuracy. Any inaccurate test could have profound influence on your reputation and ability to get a job. The problem is that it's not easy, when you are looking desperately for a job, to take a strong position against invasive testing, because your mere refusal to participate could result in your elimination. That's why it's so important for you to be cooperative, but why it's equally important for you to invest some money in protecting yourself.

The best way to protect yourself is to have an independent laboratory conduct the test. If one of the conditions for employment is that you submit to a drug check, request the right to have the test run by a laboratory of your own choosing. This will probably be rejected because if testing is a standard procedure, the firm probably has arrangements with a particular lab. So if your request is rejected, ask why, just for the record, then ask if the firm will pay for an independent test to confirm their test. If the interviewer rejects that idea, make a record of it in your notes and, if it is important enough to you, go to an independent lab and have the same test performed that the interviewer required immediately after the interviewer's test or specimen is taken. The closer your test is performed to the interviewer's test, the better.

This has two desirable results. First, you have control of the test results. If they are not in your favor you can do with them what you will. But, second, and most important, if the interviewer's test comes out not in your favor but your test comes out in your favor you are in an extremely strong position and can effectively and immediately counter any damage a negative report to your interviewer could have on your reputation.

You could also have a test done by your own lab *prior* to the interview, as close as possible to the time of your interview as is convenient. You wouldn't even have to reveal that you had the test done to the interviewer. Then you could submit to the same test with the confidence that you could rebut any unfavorable report with proof that you did not use drugs.

Non-invasive methods are being developed to check, not for drug or alcohol use, but whether or not you can safely do any potentially dangerous job. One consists of a software program in a computer operated by knobs. You use the knob to keep a swaying pointer in the center of the screen. The pointer swings faster and faster from left to right and the test ends when the pointer swings too far, as it will always do. While this doesn't test specifically for drugs or alcohol, if you are drug or alcohol impaired, you will almost invariably fail the test.

Pre-employment physical examinations. A related requirement with which you might be faced is a pre-employment examination. Both the Americans With Disabilities Act, which was signed into law in 1990 to start to take effect in July 1992 and to be fully effecive in 1994, and most state laws permit employers to use pre-employment medical examinations and to impose reasonable job standards for applicants. But there are three requirements. The medical examinations must be:

1. job related;
2. (in many states) conducted after an offer is extended; and;
3. applied uniformly to all applicants.

Additionally, California, for example, gives the applicant the right to submit the results of an independent examination if the employer's medical examination results in disqualification. Check your state's laws for a similar provision.

Many states prohibit employment discrimination on the basis of physical or mental handicap and federal law prohibits handicap discrimination by federal government contractors, subcontractors, and grant recipients. The basic issue in such cases is whether or not the handicap would affect job performance or pose a threat to others.

You may be requested to sign a consent and release form and I would be very reluctant to sign a release. You should read it very carefully. The purpose of getting you to sign a release is to avoid your making tort claims relating to the physical examination, like invasion of privacy, assault, or battery. There's generally no problem with signing a simple consent form, but a release is another matter. The problem is if you're presented with the form to sign and you don't sign it you could either be eliminated from consideration or a negative inference could be drawn from your refusal to sign that you are a troublemaker.

This is a very sensitive issue. As a matter of course I never sign releases. But I'm an attorney and I know the reason why people are asking me to sign a release. As I described earlier, I just cross off any language I don't like, initial it, and then sign the form. Sometimes the person with whom you're dealing will just take what you signed and go forward, accepting your changes. Others, however, may make an issue of it and say that they cannot proceed with processing your application unless you sign the form unchanged. That just presents you with a question of whether or not you want to sign the release. Generally nothing will happen and your signing the release will be okay. But what if something does happen? Then if you make a claim against the company, they'll pull out the release and take the position that you waived all your rights. I don't sign as a matter of principle. But then I don't need a job. It comes down to a weighing of values between your needs and the potential for harm. Generally there is very little potential for harm, so if you make a federal case out of it you might disqualify yourself for a lot of jobs for which you might otherwise be considered. So my advice would be to question the release and tell them that you don't generally sign such all-encompassing forms and ask if you can just sign the consent and cross out the release. There's a fair chance that they'll say okay. If they don't, and you're not worried about anything happening for which you might want to make a claim, then you should go ahead and sign the release and proceed with the interview.

Lie detector tests. Polygraph, or lie detector, tests were once very popular among employers as a screening device. But recently almost half the states and the District of Columbia have passed laws severely limiting the use of polygraph testing. Federal law has prohibited the use of lie detector tests as a screening device since 1988. There are a few exceptions and the federal law sometimes endorses more restrictive state laws or bargaining agreements, so if the question arises you should check your local state laws if you don't want to submit. California, for example, has a specific prohibition against employers demanding or requiring an applicant to submit to a polygraph or lie detector test as a condition of employment.

Scored testing. A very controversial method of judging job applicants involves scored testing. The law at the time of the writing of this book is that if a test or battery of tests has a "significant disparate impact" on a protected class, its use is unlawful unless it is job related. The flip side is that if the test does not have a disproportionate disparate impact on a protected class, it may be employed regardless of its validity or job relatedness. The tests for determining disparate impact are too complex to go into here. If you think you have been discriminated against because a test you took was unfairly tilted against your particular minority group, you should see an attorney who is familiar with this very complicated and litigious area of law, which is constantly changing.

CHECKLIST

★ Pre-employment questions may not be asked for the purpose of discriminating on the basis of race, color, religion, sex, national origin, age, or physical disability.

★ The EEOC views such inquiries with "extreme disfavor."

★ State laws specifically prohibit bias.

★ Most states have lists of lawful and unlawful questions.

★ If you're asked an unlawful question, answer it if your reply can't hurt you, and then let the interviewer know that you know what may and may not be asked in an interview.

★ Don't file a claim unless the purpose of the question was to discriminate for an unlawful reason.

★ You should file with both the state and the EEOC within the filing period.

★ You can file a suit in court by filing your "right to sue" letter along with an application for appointment of counsel.

★ Your remedies include damages and attorneys' fees.

★ State and local governmental employers are not immune from being ordered to pay damages because of illegal discrimination.

★ You may have to pay the other party's attorney's fees if you lose.

★ Be wary of relinquishing control over employment or health records or required pre-employment tests such as drug tests or lie-detector tests.

★ Read every document thoroughly before you sign.

★ If there's something you don't like or understand in a document you're asked to sign, discuss it with your interviewer before you sign, or cross it off and initial it.

★ Obtain a complete copy of everything you sign.

★ Initial each page of any document you sign.

★ Protect yourself by having a laboratory of your choosing perform any required invasive test, either as a substitute for your interviewer's laboratory or as a backup to protect against a false result.

DECISIONS

       Although those who write about how to conduct interviews would have us believe that hiring decisions are made empirically, the fact is that most such decisions are based on the interviewer's visceral reaction to the interviewee (and for this chapter let's assume the interviewer is a man). Sometimes this feeling is arrived at very quickly. Theodore Sorenson, who became President Kennedy's special counsel, was hired as a legislative assistant to the newly elected Senator Kennedy in 1953 after two five-minute interviews. Sometimes it comes after extensive contact.

Most decisions are made viscerally

How are decisions made? Selection decisions are no different from any other decision that we must all make. Much more often than not, decisions are made by choosing the path of least resistance. If you note the manner in which the following hundred million dollar decision was made, you'll be less impressed with the science involved in the decision-making process and less intimidated by how the decision on you is to be made.

In 1948, Henry Ford II put forth the idea of bringing out a new car. It was not until 1955, however, after exhaustive studies, that Ford made the big decision and put their final approval on the project.

A team was formed, and millions of dollars were spent in research relating to the design and marketing of the new car. One of the fundamental decisions that had to be made was what to call it. Very early it was suggested that the car be named after Henry Ford II's father, Edsel, but Ford and his brothers quickly scotched that idea, saying that they didn't believe their father would "care to have his name spinning on a million hubcaps."

So several research consultants were hired and the entire nation was canvassed. People were asked their reactions to more than two thousand names. Ford also consulted the poetess Marianne Moore, who suggested such zingers as Intelligent Bullet and Utopian Turtletop. They next went to Madison Avenue and their advertising agency, Foote, Cone & Belding, which came up with 18,000 possibilities in the twinkling of an eye (including Drof). They cut this list down to 6,000 and presented it to Ford. "There you are," an agency rep said proudly, "six thousand names, all alphabetized and cross-referenced."

"But," gasped a Ford executive, "we don't want 6,000 names. We only want one." So Foote, Cone & Belding reduced the list of 6,000 to ten and presented it to Ford's executive committee at a time when the three Ford brothers were away. The chairman of the committee looked at the ten suggestions and said, "I don't like any of them. Let's call it the Edsel." And that was that. After millions of dollars and months of research and work, the name chosen was the first one that had been suggested more than a year earlier. It was also the only one to have been categorically rejected by the top person.

And you think that the hire-no hire decision on you is going to be made scientifically? Don't kid yourself. Most decisions, regardless of the amount of money riding on them, are made viscerally.

The halo effect

The "halo" effect, which Lopez (in *Personnel Interviewing Theory and Practice*) defines as "the undue influence of an irrelevant trait on [the interviewer's] overall judgment," is probably the dominant factor in making a selection decision. The consequence of the halo effect can be devastating. I once made a terrible error that epitomizes the halo effect. I had been interviewing for a long time to fill a position in the law department for a client corporation. I simply could not find the right person for the job. Finally I interviewed a candidate who seemed right only because of a short answer to one of my questions. He was an assistant counsel in a corporation and I asked him what he did. "I don't know," he replied. "I can't tell you the specifics. All I know is that I'm always busy during the day and am always tired when I come home. I don't know why, but I just can't tell you specifically what I handle each day—but there are always a lot of people who have problems who want to see me and they always return with more problems."

I made up my mind to hire him then and there. Why? Because as a young lawyer working for Litton Industries, I had had the same problem. I was always terribly busy, people were always lining up at my door to see me, but when my friends asked me what I did, I couldn't tell them. He had expressed my feelings on the matter exactly.

Despite unanimous negative replies on my reference checks with his ex-employers, I hired him. Unfortunately, it turned out that he had irreconcilable personality defects, which verified the reference checks. But the halo I put around his answer struck such a responsive chord in me that it superseded the empirical data I compiled of an unimpressive résumé and poor reference checks to such an extent that I offered him the job.

Lopez tells how an interviewer makes a decision. I offer his insights here with the caveat that he is talking of a screening interviewer who is a scientist in the interviewing process and not a selection interviewer. But the criteria he discusses may be relevant to both.

> If the interview has been conducted properly, a great many imperfections and weaknesses will have been discovered in the applicant. If not, there was something wrong with the interview or the selection program. This unfavorable information can be quite misleading and can create a halo effect in reverse when compared to the main specification....
>
> The shrewd evaluator weighs a man's weaknesses against his strengths to arrive at an overall appraisal.... He employs a system of checks and balances, to determine what asset of the interviewee will compensate for what weakness. In any occupation, despite the allegations of some job analysts and methods engineers, there is no set pattern of requisite human attributes. Lack of formal education can be more than offset by an unusually varied and broad life experience; deficiencies in intellectual depth can be compensated for by an abundance of persistency, dedication, and energy.
>
> Some defects, of course, cannot be compensated for. A lack of ambition or drive can never be offset by a high level of intelligence or by a scintillating personality; job knowledge and skill cannot overcome personal maladjustment.

Methods of reaching a decision

In *Principles of Selling,* H. K. Nixon gives five methods of reaching a decision.

1. The method of logical reasoning.
2. The method of reason followed by voluntary decision.
3. The method of reason followed by emotional decision.
4. The method of reason followed by suggestion.
5. The method of suggestion.

Most decisions are made by methods three and four. Emotion is the most important factor in decisions made by emotional people. No matter how much logic is used, no matter how reasonable the person making the decision, the deciding factor will almost invariably be based upon emotion, a feeling.

The committee making its decision to name the car the Edsel rejected the advice of experts and made a final choice that was almost incomprehensible. They chose a name that had not been canvassed with the public, had no connotations of excitement or adventure (such as Corsair, which was the favored choice of Foote, Cone & Belding based upon their research), and had been rejected by the boss.

Why? The man who made the decision, the chairman, obviously reacted to some inner feeling he had about the other names and the one he chose. Could he define the feeling? Unlikely. Could he explain how he arrived at his decision? Doubtful. It was not arrived at through weighing empirical values. He looked at all the names and he had a feeling. "Let's call it the Edsel."

This is how you are going to be judged in your interview. The way an interviewer makes a decision on an applicant cannot be explained through logic. The interviewer will have some specific things for which he will be looking. And a candidate who does not measure up to this specification will be rejected. But the decision to make an offer will not be made simply because you fit the specification. There is something more. You must spark that feeling in him. If you do, you'll probably get an offer. If the interviewer is then asked why he made you an offer, he will most probably reply that you fit the specification for which he was looking. But that's not an accurate answer. Others fit the specification, too, but you hit that feeling and so you got the offer.

Follow-up letters

Probably the first decision you'll have to make after an interview is whether or not to write a thank-you or follow-up letter to the interviewer. One of the main points you should have learned from *Sweaty Palms* is that the vast majority of selection interviewers don't want to be conducting interviews because it interferes with their job. So anything connected with filling the position is a royal pain, and the biggest part of that pain is having to interview prospects. They want to fill the job as quickly and easily as possible, while devoting the minimum amount of time to the chore as possible. After the interview is over, the last thing they want is to receive a letter from an interviewee.

Receiving a post-interview letter can have a negative effect on an interviewer for several reasons:

1. It's a piece of paper with which they must deal. What do they do? Answer it? File it? Throw it away? If they answer it, they are probably not going to be thinking kindly of you, as you've just imposed a further burden on their time.

2. If they're not interested in you, receiving a letter from you is going to be even more of an irritant. The standard and accepted protocol for rejection is for the interviewer not to make another contact. Your letter, breaching this protocol, may negate any possibility for a change of heart.

3. It can look like you're begging or more in need of a job than the interviewer might have believed before receiving your letter.

4. Your letter might say something that negates a positive feeling the interviewer may have formed.

5. It reduces the control of the situation that the interviewer might feel he has. The interviewer has the control of when and how to make further contact. If the interviewee oversteps the bounds by making the first contact after the interview, it could make the interviewer feel he has to reply and he might not feel he's in a position to reply just at that time. So if he has to make a decision before he wants to, the odds are that the decision will be negative.

An interviewer won't contact you unless he's interested in you, regardless of whether or not you write a letter, so, unless you know for certain that you've been rejected, writing a letter subjects you to the risk of damaging your position. The interviewer knows that you are grateful for the interview, so you don't need to tell him that. He also knows that anything in a letter is probably insincere with the ulterior motive of getting an offer or another interview. Because of that very real fact, a follow-up letter is a very difficult document to draft. There's not much you can say that doesn't sound hypocritical to the reader who will be reading the letter with a far different perspective than the perspective from which you wrote it.

Finally, there is no question of courtesy involved here. You are in a business environment. The interviewer didn't do you any favors by granting you an interview. He was acting out of selfish motives because he has a position to fill, so you do not have an obligation to "thank" him for the interview.

There are three exceptions to this advice. The first is if the interviewer has asked you for additional information. That gives you an opening to provide the information and write a letter that could enhance your position. The second is when you know that you have been rejected in the interview. If you've been told that you won't be considered further, then you've got nothing to lose by making an additional contact. The employer might change his mind or refer you to another firm. The third exception is if the interview has been conducted over a meal. Then it might be appropriate to write a very short, polite note of thanks for the meal if the interviewer picked up the tab. It's not necessary to write a thank-you note because the meal was part of the interview process, but this does give you the flexibility of making contact without breaching protocol and without looking insincere or hypocritical. If you do wish to write a note, limit it to a few words of thanks. Don't grovel about how much you'd like the job or how much you liked the interviewer's tie or what a terrific sense of humor the interviewer has. Don't mention the job or include the lamentable "I look forward to hearing from you." Just thank him for the meal and end it.

The final decision

You must make a decision, too. Do you want to accept a position if it's offered? Often, interviewees use a halo principle in accepting or rejecting an offer. Perhaps the classic story epitomizing this was told to me by an executive of a major corporation. She had been interviewing for an employee and found someone she liked and offered her the job. The lady rejected it because of the "left turns." The executive asked what she meant and the interviewee replied that in order to get to work she would have to make a left turn and she didn't want any job where she'd have to make a left turn every day because she wasn't good at making left turns!

You should be able to make a decision based on more relevant arguments (or be able to perceive obvious solutions like three right turns in lieu of the one offending left turn). You can use the principles set forth in this chapter, but basically it comes down to two factors. The first is whether or not the job offered meets your requirements which you determined in Chapter 2. If it does, or if it meets them with variations with which you can live, consider the second factor: What kind of "feeling" do you have about the job? Do you like the person for whom you will be working? If not, can you get along with the person for whom you will be working, even though you might not like him? How intense is your feeling? Is it dislike, or is it ambivalence? If it's ambivalence, then there shouldn't be a problem working for him and maybe the ambivalence will change to respect, if not affection. But if your feelings are a dislike of the person, you would be starting out with two strikes against your chances for success.

In evaluating your feeling for your potential employer, you must be honest with yourself as to how well you did in the interview, and this points up the importance of going into the interview feeling that you are also the interviewer. If you were able to probe the areas of your interviewer's personality that could affect your on-the-job relationship, then you should have a fairly confident opinion of how you feel about him. If you did not conduct a good interview, just went along with no control or confidence, then you're taking a crap shoot on your feelings.

If the interview was less than conclusive, you still have several alternatives. You could just reject the offer and not take the chance of a personality conflict. You could take the job and hope that when you get better acquainted things will work out. Or you could ask for another interview with the person, at which time you could probe on a more personal level to test your feelings.

One point in favor of accepting the position is that the mere fact of being offered the job signifies that the interviewer looks upon you with strong positive feelings. This could be an indication that any ambivalent or negative feelings you have might not be accurate and that the job could work out quite well for you.

EPILOGUE

$\mathbf{F}$ollowing is a letter I received from reader Diane Slack in Columbia, Maryland. In it she eloquently covers many of the points raised in *Sweaty Palms* that should be of interest to all interviewees, especially women. I am including her letter here because it is an excellent example of how a good interviewee should approach the interview and handle various problems that can arise in the interview situation.

Dear Mr. Medley,

Your book...was so helpful I had to write and thank you. I found your book full of useful suggestions, sound philosophies, and delightful humor and anecdotes. It was a pleasure to read and a useful tool.

Understanding that the interviewer controls the interview through content was the single most beneficial point made for my use. It represents a challenge and demands an assertive spirit. By looking at an opportunity on a more self-controlled level, I feel more confident. Being recently graduated, young, and female, I often feel intimidated by an interviewer's strong personality. I found, when I went through on-campus interviews, those interviewers were well-seasoned in their positions. Others may be less intimidating.

Many interviewers see a college graduate as an inexperienced, entry-level-only applicant. They seem to ignore the qualities that led that person into college in the first place. Why would a college graduate jump at a job that a person with a high school diploma could easily do? Employers must realize that many college graduates seek [more of a] challenge. . . . [Most] personnel workers can't comprehend readily why I might take a lower-paying job that offers more variety, responsibility, or exposure. In an interview they try to outguess what you want to do. They assume inexperience and youthful passivity. The interviewee must speak up, stop the wrong direction of the interview, and ask for what they want even if it means that the company may reply that they don't have such a position at that time. I even went so far (after getting the confidence from your book) as to be up-front and tactfully say that in a few months I would be bored or get restless with the position. This finally made what I was trying to convey sink in with the interviewer. She paused. I didn't let the silence bother me. Then she gave me an acknowledging nod. Rather than take offense, she actually admired my honesty. She wanted me with her company. Now we just had to find a job that would fit.

That afternoon I interviewed for three positions. The last one was what I was looking for and I had a job offer right during the interview. What a boost to the ego. What a compliment! The company wanted me so much that they took all afternoon getting to know me and had me talk with a total of five people. If they didn't want me on their "team," they wouldn't have given me the time of day. But I had convinced them I was an asset worth working to get.

I'd like to describe a few other experiences I had. . . .

1. Realizing I didn't want the job. I got an interview for a "management trainee position" in the credit department of a retail store. Within the first ten minutes of the interview I had learned about the job and, through questioning the interviewer, found

that the "program" was completed in an average of three to five years on the job. In effect, this meant that you started as a clerk, just as a high school graduate would, and moved up in the company just like any other employee. They had actually invented the "management trainee" title just to attract college graduates. There were no seminars or classes, no mentor program, etc. In effect, all clerks were "management trainees" because, in due time, if they were qualified, they'd get promoted.

I was offended because I felt I had been led there under false pretenses. I was in an interview for a job I didn't want, and the interviewer was continuing this uncomfortable situation by arranging a second interview with her superior. I ended up sticking with it and answering questions politely, hoping it wouldn't be long before I could get out of there. If I had been brave enough, I would have called a halt to it. . . . I would have saved everyone's time and spared myself the feeling of insincerity during the second interview. It's hard to appear interested when you're not.

2. The "swinger." Here we go with assumptions again. The president of this company used analogies he thought I could relate to, like "if I were to try to pick you up at a bar" and "us meeting at a party," etc. He even made a point of telling me he was recently divorced. I think he was trying to project a "swinger" image. I was offended. He had assumed, because I was young, female, and single, that I sat in bars waiting for a man to drop me a line, for a pick-up. And here he had my résumé right in front of him, my grades, academic accomplishments, degree, and work experience. It turned my stomach. I directed all energies to bringing the interview around to professionalism, thanked him for his time, and left, knowing I didn't want to work with this man. He showed lack of respect for me.

3. The gamers. I went through an interview with a woman whom I greatly admired because of her actions during the interview. She was professional, intelligent, qualified for her own job, etc. The interview went really well. I was pretty sure she'd be making me an offer. I was even more sure when she took me to meet the men I'd be working for. At this point I knew enough about the company and the position to really want the job and the opportunity it represented. Then I met the two men. I was left sitting between them. I sat and answered their questions politely and honestly. We were getting to know each other. Then they started asking strange questions. What's your favorite color? Your favorite number? Which of these figures

I've drawn do you like best? Least? Can you be teased? Are you a crier? They asked if I had heard of an eighteenth-century Russian economist, and pretended to be surprised when I hadn't. It was harassment. Then they laughed and admitted they were teasing me.... They kept repeating how stressful the job was, and I kept thinking how much of that stress was created by non-job-related sources. When I left, I started thinking about how unprofessional my interview had been. And those two would be my bosses! I declined the offer and went with a company that has a professional image and treats its employees as unique, special, and human assets to the company. No one needs outside harassment. Most jobs provide enough conflicts each day to deal with.

Well, I guess that's the extent of my job-seeking experiences. Thanks again. Your book helped me with phobia sensations I had—the concept that the interviewee controls the content of the interview helped me build enough confidence to express my ideas and my desires rather than, as you say, being a passive patsy, waiting for a crumb from the table. It made me realize that it was all right to be assertive, and that maybe because of this behavior, communication during the interview would actually be improved. I went through several interviews wherein I felt intimidated by the interviewer and politely answered the questions asked of me, patiently waiting till they asked the right one, so I could tell them what I really wanted them to know about me. Now I realize that I can take over some of the direction of the questioning by answering in particular ways. This sense of control puts me at ease and allows me to think about what to mention that will fit the job duties best, and how to get the right message across to the interviewer. I believe it is confidence that is so important in selling yourself and getting the best match between you and the job.

APPENDIX A
COMMONLY ASKED QUESTIONS

This appendix consists of three sections of questions commonly asked in the selection interview. The first section contains questions reported by 242 companies surveyed for the *Northwestern Lindquist-Endicott Report* by Victor R. Lindquist, published and copyrighted by The Placement Center, Northwestern University, Evanston, Illinois. The second section contains questions suggested by Walter R. Mahler in his book *How Effective Executives Interview.* Questions in this section are usually used when interviewing people already in the job market. The third section sets forth additional questions that can pop up in an interview and for which an interviewee should be prepared.

You can expect to be asked some of the questions in this appendix in an interview. Some are unlawful. I suggest that you go through a mock interview and have these questions shot at you at random in any order chosen by your mock interviewer. These questions present starting points. You should encourage your mock interviewer to ask follow-up questions not on this list, to press you, to impose stress, and to ask more difficult questions if they pop into the interviewer's head, because that's the way your selection interviewer will operate. With preparation such as this, it is less likely that you'll be caught unaware in an actual interview.

Section I: Assessment questions asked by professional interviewers

1. What goals have you set for yourself? How are you planning to achieve them?

2. Who or what has had the greatest influence on the development of your career interests?

3. What factors did you consider in choosing your major?

4. Why are you interested in our organization?

5. Tell me about yourself.

6. What two or three things are most important to you in a position?

7. What kind of work do you want to do?

8. Tell me about a project you initiated.

9. What are your expectations of your future employer?

10. What is your GPA? How do you feel about it? Does it reflect your ability?

11. How do you solve conflicts?

12. Tell me about how you perceive your strengths. Your weaknesses. How do you evaluate yourself?

13. What work experience has been the most valuable to you and why?

14. What was the most useful criticism you ever received, and who was it from?

15. Give an example of a problem you have solved and the process you used.

16. Describe the project or situation that best demonstrated your analytical skills.

17. What has been your greatest challenge?

18. Describe a situation where you had a conflict with another individual, and how you dealt with it.

19. What were the biggest problems you have encountered in college? How have you handled them? What did you learn from them?

20. What are your team-player qualities? Give examples.

21. Describe your leadership style.

22. What interests or concerns you about the position or the company?

23. In a particular leadership role you had, what was the greatest challenge?

24. What idea have you developed and implemented that was particularly creative or innovative?

25. What characteristics do you think are important for this position?

26. How have your educational and work experiences prepared you for this position?

27. Take me through a project where you demonstrated_____ skills.

28. How do you think you have changed personally since you started college?

29. Tell me about a team project of which you are particularly proud and your contribution.

30. How do you motivate people?

31. Why did you choose the extracurricular activities you did? What did you gain? What did you contribute?

32. What types of situations put you under pressure, and how do you deal with the pressure?

33. Tell me about a difficult decision you have made.

34. Give an example of a situation in which you failed, and how you handled it.

35. Tell me about a situation when you had to persuade another person to your point of view.

36. What frustrates you the most?

37. Knowing what you know now about your college experience, would you make the same decisions?

38. What can you contribute to this company?

39. How would you react to having your credibility questioned?

40. What characteristics are most important in a good manager? How have you displayed one of these characteristics?

41. What challenges are you looking for in a position?

42. Are you willing to relocate or travel as part of your career?

43. What two or three accomplishments have given you the most satisfaction?

44. Describe a leadership role of yours and tell why you committed your time to it.

45. How are you conducting your job search, and how will you make your decision?

46. What is the most important lesson you have learned in or out of school?

47. Describe a situation where you had to work with someone who was difficult. How was the person difficult, and how did you handle it?

48. We are looking at a lot of great candidates; why are you the best person for this position?

49. How would your friends describe you? Your professors?

50. What else should I know about you?

These questions reflect a significant movement away from standard directive questions toward more open-ended situational queries. Common themes include applications of analytical, problem-solving and decision-making skills, leadership development, creativity, teamwork, and personal development.

Section II

1. Beginning with your move into your first supervisory job, would you tell me briefly why each change was made?

2. Referring to your most recent position, what would you say are some of your more important accomplishments? I'd be interested in operating results and any other accomplishments you consider important. (Probe four or five accomplishments. Get specific data.)

3. Considering these accomplishments, what are some of the reasons for your success?

4. Were there any unusual difficulties you had to overcome in getting these accomplishments?

5. What two or three things do you feel you have learned on this job?

6. What did you particularly like about the position?

7. There are always a few negatives about a position. What would you say you liked least about the position?

8. What responsibilities or results have not come up to your expectations? I'd be interested in things you had hoped and planned to accomplish which were not done. I sometimes call them disappointments. (Push for several specific answers.)

9. What are some of the reasons for this?

10. I'm interested in how you do your planning. What planning processes have you found useful, and how do you go about them?

11. In what way do you feel you have improved in your planning in the last few years?

12. What are some examples of important types of decisions or recommendations you are called upon to make?

13. Would you describe how you went about making these types of decisions or recommendations? With whom did you talk, and so forth?

14. What decisions are easiest for you to make and which ones are more difficult?

15. Most of us can think of an important decision which we would make quite differently if we made it again. Any examples from your experience? Probe: What's the biggest mistake you can recall?

16. Most of us improve in our decision-making ability as we get greater experience. In what respects do you feel you have improved in your decision making?

17. What has been your experience with major expansion or reduction of force? (Explore for details.)

18. How many immediate subordinates have you selected in the past two years? How did you go about it? Any surprises or disappointments?

19. How many immediate subordinates have you removed from their jobs in the last few years? Any contemplated? One example of how you went about it.

20. How do you feel your subordinates would describe you as a delegator? Any deliberate tactics you use?

21. Some managers keep a very close check on their organization. Others use a loose rein. What pattern do you follow? How has it changed in the last few years?

22. What has been the most important surprise you have received from something getting out of control? Why did it happen?

23. Let's talk about standards of performance. How would you describe your own? What would your subordinates say? What would your boss say?

24. Sometimes it is necessary to issue an edict to an individual or

the entire staff. Do you have any recent examples of edicts you have issued? Probe: Reasons? Results?

25. What things do you think contribute to your effectiveness as a supervisor?

26. From an opposite viewpoint, what do you think might interfere with your effectiveness as a supervisor?

27. In what respects do you feel you have improved most as a supervisor during the last few years?

28. What kind of supervisor gets the best performance out of you?

29. Some managers are quite deliberate about such things as communications, development, and motivation. Do you have any examples of how you do this?

30. What have you done about your own development in the last few years?

31. Would you describe your relationship with your last three supervisors?

32. Considering your relationships both inside and outside the component, would you give me an example of how you have been particularly effective in relating with others?

33. Would you also give me an example of how you might not have been particularly effective in relating with others?

34. Some people are short-fused and impatient in their reactions. How would you describe yourself?

35. Have you encountered any health problems? What do you do about your health?

36. Most of us can look back upon a new idea, a new project, or an innovation we feel proud introducing. Would you describe one or two such innovations you are particularly proud of?

37. How do you feel about your progress (career-wise) to date?

38. What are your aspirations for the future? Have these changed?

39. We sometimes compare the assets and limitations of our products with competition. Let's do a related thing with your career. Thinking of your competition for jobs to which you aspire, what would you say are your limitations? (Get three or more assets and three or more limitations.)

40. Are there any conditions of personal business, health, or family which would limit your flexibility for taking on a new assignment?

Section III: General questions

1. Tell me about yourself.
2. What was your favorite subject in school? Why?
3. What was your least favorite subject in school? Why?
4. What were your grades/class standing?
5. Why did you go to the school you attended?
6. How did you choose your major/course of study?
7. What extra-curricular activities did you participate in school?
8. Did you have a favorite teacher?
9. Why did you like this teacher better than anyone else?
10. What have you accomplished so far in life?
11. What have you done of which you're most proud? Why?
12. What's your best asset?
13. What's your biggest weakness?
14. Have you ever been arrested?
15. Have you ever been convicted of a crime?
16. How do you get along with people?
17. What are your outside interests/activities?
18. Do they interfere with your job?
19. Have you ever told a lie? Explain.
20. Why do you want to work for us?
21. How would you handle an irate/irrational customer?
22. What is a good (whatever job you're applying for, e.g., secretary)?
23. What's the most difficult task you've ever undertaken? How did it work out?
24. What can you do for us?
25. Why should we hire you?
26. What can I do for you?
27. Why do you feel you are qualified for this job?
28. Does your present employer know you're interviewing for another job?
29. Why do you want to change jobs?
30. Did you have any problems in any of your previous jobs?

31. What do you think you'll be doing in ten years?

32. What would you like to be doing in ten years?

33. What do you want to accomplish in life?

34. If money were not a consideration, what would you want to do?

35. Do you consider yourself a professional? Why (not)?

36. Who/what has been the greatest influence in your life? Why?

37. How do you get along with your parents?

38. Do you prefer one of your parents over the other? Why?

39. Have you ever been fired?

40. Do you drink alcoholic beverages?

41. Have you ever used drugs?

42. Will you submit to a drug/blood test?

43. Do you think there's any correlation between grades in school and success on the job?

44. Who paid for your education?

45. If you were starting over again right now, what would you do?

46. Do you have a boy/girlfriend? Do you live together?

47. What's your sexual preference?

48. Are you married?

49. How old are you?

50. Are you in good health?

51. Is there anything that you haven't revealed, either in this interview or on your résumé, that would affect our decision?

52. Have you had any other interviews? With whom?

53. What did you do to prepare for this interview?

54. Have you ever been rejected? How did you react/handle it?

55. Have you ever been passed over for promotion? How did you react/handle it?

56. How much money are you making now?

57. How much money do you want?

58. How much money do you think you'll be making in five years?

59. What did your father do?

60. Is your private life happy? Why (not)?

61. Are you a happy person?

62. Are you satisfied?

63. What makes you angry?

64. What's your net worth?

65. What's your social security number?

66. How well do you take criticism?

67. Have you ever supervised anyone? Explain.

68. Do you like to travel?

69. Do you have a family?

70. Do you plan on having any (more) children?

71. How do you feel about (any controversial issue, like the death penalty)?

72. Do you read? What? How often?

73. What magazines do you read regularly?

74. What's the last book you read?

75. Do you watch a lot of television/go to movies?

76. What's your favorite movie/book/TV show? Why?

77. How do you keep in shape?

78. What salary do you want?

79. Why do you think you're worth that?

80. Would you be willing to work for less?

81. Is money the most important aspect of a job for you?

82. Do you require close supervision?

83. Have you always been treated fairly?

84. Give me three references I can talk to about you.

85. Please sign this release so we can talk to your references about you.

86. What's the most important thing you're looking for in a job/employer?

87. Do you like people?

88. Have you ever done anything you regret?

89. Describe your character.

90. Have you ever done anything of which you're ashamed?

91. Have you ever been reprimanded?

92. Do you work better alone or with people?

93. Do you think you are unique? How?

94. Tell me about your present job.

95. How do you spend most of your time in your present job?

96. How do you feel about your job/employer?

97. Where do you rank your present job with others you've held? Why?

98. Is there anything about your present job/employer you'd change or of which you are critical?

99. How many hours a day do you think a person should spend on the job?

100. Do you devote any time or money to charity work?

101. What do you feel is an acceptable attendance record?

102. Do you arrive on time?

103. What do you think about your present supervisor/hair job/employer?

104. What do you think are your present supervisor's strengths and weaknesses?

105. How does your present supervisor treat others in your department?

106. What are your goals?

107. What have you done that indicates you are qualified for this job?

108. How do you think you should be judged on the job?

109. Do you go to church/synagogue/temple/mosque?

110. Are you tolerant of different people/opinions?

111. How long would you plan to work for us?

112. Do you like to travel?

113. Is there any section of the country in which you'd prefer to live/work? Why?

114. Have you always done your best?

115. Are you an overachiever or an underachiever? Explain.

116. Do you have any questions?

APPENDIX B
EVALUATION FACTORS USED BY
INTERVIEWERS

This appendix consists of a list of interview turnoffs reported by interviewers in 320 business and industrial organizations who were surveyed for the *Northwestern Lindquist-Endicott Report* by Victor R. Lindquist, published and copyrighted by The Placement Center, Northwestern University, Evanston, Illinois. Manifestation of any of these factors could create a negative impression and ultimately lead to rejection.

Interview "turnoffs"

What behavior, response, or activity by a job applicant to you as an interviewer is an immediate "turnoff"?

1. Arrogance/cockiness
2. Poor oral communication/presentation skills
3. Lack of interest
4. Lack of knowledge about the industry
5. Early discussion or questions about salary/benefits
6. Being unprepared for interviews and making excuses
7. Egotism/overconfidence
8. Tardiness/not showing up for interview
9. Poor eye contact
10. Abrasive/rude/demanding
11. Dishonesty/fabricated answers in interview or résumé
12. Poor language usage/slang/poor grammar
13. No career direction/not knowing self
14. Shallow/inappropriate questions or answers
15. Lack of experience/education/activities/skills
16. Lack of professional appearance

17. "Know-it-all" attitude
18. Inappropriate attire
19. Unrealistic goals, career, and job expectations
20. Overly aggressive/hostile/manipulative behavior
21. Lack of enthusiasm
22. Poor grooming/hygiene
23. Does not communicate qualifications effectively/no elaboration or examples
24. Deficient social skills/lack of interpersonal skills/poor conversational skills
25. Lack of professionalism and poise
26. Evasive/vague responses to specific questions
27. Not listening
28. Loud/talks too much/rambles
29. Unprofessional/poor attitude
30. Extremely shy individuals
31. Lack of questions
32. Racist/prejudiced/sexist remarks
33. No initiative/unassertive/passive
34. Lack of intelligence/poor academic record
35. Unwillingness to relocate
36. Uncommunicative/nonresponsive
37. Negativism
38. Lack of self-confidence/defeatist
39. Condescending/patronizing
40. More interested in what company can do for them
41. Adverse body language/poor posture and expressions
42. Lack of energy/falling asleep
43. Expect interviewer to tell them about the company
44. Lack of knowledge about the company
45. Inability to show their interest and why they are qualified
46. Distracted/not paying attention
47. Immature behavior/cutesy

48. Foul/abusive language

49. Evidence of weak teamwork or other leadership skills

50. Negative comments regarding supervisors, co-workers, or faculty

51. Overstating qualifications

52. Disclosure of immoral, illegal, or unethical behavior

53. Lazy/lax attitude

54. Personality problems/psychotic behavior

55. Extreme nervousness

56. Inappropriate, impolite behavior

57. Poor quality/mistakes on résumé or applications

58. Gum chewing or smoking

59. Overfamiliarity with recruiter

60. Inflexibility

61. Lack of fit between candidate's qualifications/career goals and job specifications

62. "Shopping the market"/practice interviewing

63. Inability to communicate or comprehend clearly in English

64. Treating personnel professional as "trial to be endured"

65. Insensitivity to the interview transaction

66. Poor writing skills

67. Appearing to be drunk or on drugs

68. Inconsistency

69. Canned responses

70. Lack of desire to learn

Content issues, such as a lack of knowledge about the company, comprise the largest "turnoff" (32%). Other themes include attitude (29%), behavior (18%), communication (16%), and appearance (5%). Many of the "turnoffs" are easily addressed through careful preparation for interviews and the job search. Other factors, especially the attitudes cited, are more subjective, and many candidates are likely to be unaware that they are losing the interviewer. Mock interviews, feedback, and assistance from placement professionals should help to bridge this perception gap.

Interviewees are also turned off by interviewers who are unenthusiastic, unprofessional, or lack good listening skills. Interviewers should realize that these same behaviors and attitudes may cause an interviewee to be "turned off" and be lost as a prospect.

APPENDIX C
QUESTIONS ASKED BY INTERVIEWERS WHEN THEY CHECK YOUR REFERENCES

An interviewee should be aware that a reference check may be made on him at some time during the interview process. These are some of the questions that may be asked. Numbers 8 and 9 are catch-alls. They can elicit responses relating to the candidate's moral character or other sensitive areas that an interviewer may not wish to query specifically. Number 10 is a method to get references from people not suggested by the interviewee. Interviewers recognize that an interviewee is not going to suggest as a reference one who will not give a good one. Therefore, by having the reference name some other references, the interviewer is getting a more objective source—one who has not been preconditioned by the interviewee.

1. How long did the applicant work for you?
2. What was the quality of the work?
3. How much responsibility did the applicant have?
4. How did the applicant get along with people?
5. Did the applicant require close supervision?
6. Was the applicant prompt?
7. Why did the applicant leave your company?
8. Do you know of anything that would disqualify the applicant for the job we're considering hiring the applicant for?
9. Can you think of anything I should know about the applicant that I haven't asked about?
10. Do you know anyone else to whom I could speak about the applicant?

APPENDIX D
QUESTIONS TO ASK OF THE
INTERVIEWER

Following is a list of questions suggested by William R. Nolan, founding director of the Institute for Executive Career Management in Toronto, Ontario, Canada. Some of these questions will only be appropriate at later stages of the interview process and, if asked too soon, could be offensive to the interviewer. But you should review them prior to your first interview because not only do they give you some good questions to ask if you are asked if you have any, a thorough review of them could help clarify your personal feelings about what you want in a job.

One caveat: in asking a question you should know why you want the answer. If you ask a question merely for the sake of asking the question and have no reason for wanting the knowledge, you risk looking foolish. A smart interviewer will spot an idle question right away. For instance, if you ask "How long has present management been in control?" the interviewer might ask you why you want to know that and what possible difference that makes to whether or not you take the job. If you don't have a good reason, you will be in a very difficult position and the pain you feel will be you kicking yourself for having asked the question. So for each question you ask, be sure you have a reason for asking in case you're challenged.

Job Specifications:
1. What are the duties and responsibilities for this position?
2. How can the job be altered and upgraded?

Job History:
1. How long has the position been in existence?
2. [How long has the position been] open?
3. Who had the job until now?
4. Did he or she succeed or fail?

5. What led to the success or failure?
6. How many preceded?
7. What happened to them? Why?

Personnel:

1. Who are the people—immediate superior, subordinates, associates in related departments—with whom I will be working?
2. What are their titles, history with the company, previous background, education, etc?
3. Any helpful suggestions?

The Organization:

1. Where does this position fit into the company's organization plan?
2. What are the reporting channels?
3. To whom will I be accountable (more than one boss?)?

Orientation Training:

1. Does the company have an orientation program for new employees?
2. How do I become familiar with company policies, practice, and etiquette?
3. Does the company have an executive development program?
4. Other training programs?
5. What are its facilities?
6. What resources does it utilize?
7. Does the company sponsor courses at universities? At management associations or industry conferences?
8. Are suggestions welcomed?

The Company:

1. How long has the company been in existence?
2. Who owns it? Family dominated?
3. How long has its present management been in control?
4. What is its management/operating style?
5. What has been its gross sales and profit (or loss) pattern during the last 10 years? Five years? Two years? Now?

6. Does the company have a growth plan?

7. (See annual report.) What do the company's annual report and the Dunn & Bradstreet report show about its credit rating and financial history?

8. If the company is public what do recent stockbroker's reports say about its management and its prospects? How does the company rate in the industry? What is the economic trend of the industry?

The Community:

1. Where can I get information on housing, cost of living, religious, social organizations, shopping, community, schools, libraries, educational and recreational facilities, etc?

2. Does the company dominate the community? Social life?

Compensation, Advancement:

1. Does the company offer stock options or deferred payment plans? Bonus arrangements?

2. What is the executive package at top levels?

3. Does the company reimburse moving expenses? Losses incurred in selling one's house? Living and travel expenses while employee is commuting and finding permanent housing for his/her family?

4. Does the company arrange employment contacts?

5. What is the company's policy regarding vacation and sick leave?

6. What is the company's policy regarding international tax matters?

7. Is tax and legal advice available where "international" payments are involved?

8. When and how is the salary usually paid?

9. What is the company's policy regarding agency fees?

10. Does the company have a periodic employee appraisal or performance review?

11. What are the prospects for salary increase? Promotions?

12. Will there be opportunities for greater responsibility and broader experience?

BIBLIOGRAPHY

Alvarez, Walter C. *Nervousness & Indigestion.* 3rd ed. Collier Books, 1967.

Ambrose, Stephen E. *The Supreme Commander.* Doubleday & Co., 1970.

Andrews, Colman, *Los Angeles Times,* July 19, 1987, "The waiting game may be only a state of mind."

Bach, George R., & Deutsch, Ronald M. *Pairing.* Avon Books, 1971.

Baker, Carlos. *Ernest Hemingway: A Life Story.* Charles Scribner's Sons, 1969.

Baldridge, Letitia. *The Amy Vanderbilt Complete Book of Etiquette.* Doubleday & Co., 1978.

Bellows, Roger M., *Employment Psychology: The Interview.* Rinehart & Company, 1954.

Bernstein, Harry, *Los Angeles Times,* December 25, 1990, "Performance Tests vs Drug Tests."

Birren, Faber. *Color in Your World.* Crowell-Collier, 1962.

Brooks, John. "The Fate of the Edsel." In *Great Business Disasters,* edited by Isadora Barmash. Ballantine Books, 1973.

California Lawyer, April 1982, "All About Sleep."

Capra, Frank. *The Name Above the Title.* Macmillan, 1971.

Carnegie, Dale. *How to Win Friends and Influence People.* Simon & Schuster, 1936.

Davies, Hunter. *The Beatles.* Dell, 1968.

Fast Julius. *Body Language.* Pocket Books, 1971.

Fenlason, Anne F. *Essentials in Interviewing.* Harper & Bros., 1952.

Fraser, John Munro. *A Handbook of Employment Interviewing.* 3rd ed. Macdonald & Evans, 1954.

— — . *Employment Interviewing.* 4th ed. Macdonald & Evans, 1966.

Gallwey, W. Timothy. *The Inner Game.* Random House, 1974.

Griffith, Thomas. "Newswatch." *Time.* November 8, 1976.

Halberstam, David. *The Best and the Brightest.* Random House, 1969.

Harriman, W. Averell, and Abel, Ellie. *Special Envoy to Churchill & Stalin.* Random House, 1975.

Honig, Donald H. *Baseball: When the Grass Was Real.* Coward, McCann & Geaghegan, 1975.

Ivey, Paul W. *Successful Salesmanship.* 6th ed. Prentice-Hall, 1942.

Jameson, Robert. *The Professional Job Changing System.* 4th ed., rev. Performance Dynamics, 1976.

Lay, Beirne, Jr. *Someone Has to Make It Happen.* Prentice-Hall, 1969.

Bibliography

Lindquist, Victor R. *Northwestern Lindquist-Endicott Report.* The Placement Center, Northwestern University.

Lopez, Felix M., Jr. *Personnel Interviewing Theory and Practice.* McGraw-Hill Book Company, 1965.

Los Angeles Magazine, December, 1986, "Insider."

Lundgren, Hal. "Injury Effects Still Plague Greene," *The Sporting News.* November 13, 1976.

Mahler, Walter R. *How Effective Executives Interview.* Dow-Jones-Irwin, 1976.

Maltz, Maxwell. *Psycho-Cybernetics.* Pocket Books, 1966.

Martin, Judith. *Miss Manners' Guide to Excruciatingly Correct Behavior.* Atheneum, 1982.

Medley, H. Anthony. *UCLA Basketball: The Real Story.* Galant Press, 1972.

Nixon, H. K. *Principles of Selling.* McGraw-Hill Co., 1931.

Oldfield, R. C. *The Psychology of the Interview.* 4th ed. Methuen & Co., 1951.

Peale, Norman Vincent. *The Power of Positive Thinking.* Prentice-Hall, 1952.

Pogue, Forrest C. *George C. Marshall: Ordeal and Hope.* Viking Press, 1966.

Rancho News, February 14, 1991, "Salaries for Office Help Low."

Rapaport, Ron. "A Man Has to Fear What's Down the Road." *Los Angeles Times.* November 2, 1976.

Rickenbacker, Edward V. *Rickenbacker.* Prentice Hall, 1967.

Schuller, Robert H. *Move Ahead with Possibility Thinking.* Fleming H. Revell, 1975.

Sorensen, Theodore C. *Kennedy.* Harper & Row, 1965.

Thomas, Bob. *Thalberg.* Doubleday, 1969.

Time Magazine, May 9, 1983, "Embellishment Yes, Lying No."

Turnbull, Andrew (editor). *The Letters of F. Scott Fitzgerald.* Charles Scribner's Sons, 1963.

Walters, Barbara. *How to Talk with Practically Anybody about Practically Anything.* Doubleday, 1970.

Weinland, James D., and Gross, Margaret V. *Personnel Interviewing.* Ronald Press Company, 1952.

Woolf, Bob. *Friendly Persuasion.* G. P. Putnam's Sons, New York, —.

Zunin, Leonard, with Zunin, Natalie. *Contact — The First Four Minutes.* Nash Publishing Company, 1972.

INDEX

Index

NOTES

NOTES

NOTES

NOTES

NOTES

More career books from Ten Speed Press:

WHAT COLOR IS YOUR PARACHUTE? by Richard N. Bolles
This classic in the career field is substantially revised and updated every year. Practical advice, step-by-tep exercises, and a warm, human tone make it *the* guide for job-hunters and career changers. "The giant title in the field"—*New York Times.* $12.95 paper, 425 pages

WHO'S HIRING WHO by Richard Lathrop
Fully revised and updated version of a career book highly recommended by Richard Bolles. Practical, hands-on methods for scouting the job market, presenting any and all experience in the best light, and landing the right job at the right salary. $9.95 paper, 268 pages

THE RIGHT PLACE AT THE RIGHT TIME by Robert Wegmann and Robert Chapman
A systematic, structured approach to job-hunting, covering self-evaluation, research, and interviewing. "It takes much of the drudgery out of the hunt and puts some excitement in."—*The Christian Science Monitor.* $11.95 paper, 192 pages

JOB AND CAREER BUILDING by Richard Germann & Peter Arnold
"One of the very best books (on) how to approach and sell yourself to employers once you know what it is you want to do."—Richard Bolles, author of WHAT COLOR IS YOUR PARACHUTE? Successful careers don't just happen— this book shows how to plan and attain the most satisfying career path for you. $7.95 paper, 256 pages.

THE OVERNIGHT RESUME by Donald Asher
Tricks of the trade from the president of Resume Righters, the largest resume writing office in the world, enable anyone to write a hard-hitting, fast-track resume overnight. Includes special sections on common resume problems and how to avoid them, job search protocol, and unique resume styles— medical, law, finance, and academic. $7.95 paper, 136 pages.

THE DAMN GOOD RESUME GUIDE by Yana Parker
Our bestselling resume book, updated with 22 all-new functional-style resumes. Shows how to turn your resume into a vital self-marketing tool, not just a boring list of jobs. Section on informational interviewing, targeting your resume to your job objective, and integrating work and non-work experience $6.95 paper, 80 pages.

Available from your local bookstore, or order direct from the publisher. Please include $1.25 shipping & handling for the first book, and 50 cents for each additional book. California residents include local sales tax. Write for our free complete catalog of over 400 books and tapes.

Ten Speed Press
Box 7123
Berkeley, CA 94707
(510) 845-8414

Now you can listen to Sweaty Palms interviews!

This tape dramatizes the interview situations you've read about in *Sweaty Palms*. You'll hear the goof-ups, the blunders, and examples of everything you should avoid in an interview. This audio version of the book is the fastest, most efficient way to refresh yourself on the principles of good interviewing and avoiding sweaty palms—you may even want to listen to it in your car as your drive to interviews.

If you liked the book, you'll love the audio!

Available from your local bookstore, or order using the form below. Tapes cost $12.95, plus $3.95 shipping & handling. California residents include local sales tax. Make your check out to Galant Press.

Please send me _____ copies of the Sweaty Palms audio tape.

_____

Name

_____

Address

_____

City   State   Zip

Sweaty Palms Audio Tape
c/o H. Anthony Medley
P.O. Box 9723
Marina del Rey, CA 90925

Please allow 4-6 weeks for delivery